Millbrook

– the Hidden Past

Millbrook

– the Hidden Past

ROSALEEN WILKINSON

ISBN: 0 9532830 1 1

Published by Rosaleen Wilkinson
Typeset by Andover Printing Company
and printed by Hobbs The Printers, Totton, Hampshire

Contents

ABOUT THE AUTHOR

Rosaleen Wilkinson is a lifelong resident of Southampton, being educated at Bitterne Church of England Juniors and The Atherley School. A graduate in Social and Economic History of the University of Exeter, she developed an interest in Local History when she gave up teaching in Special Education to bring up her family.

Cover pictures:

FRONT COVER

Top left: **Maritime Freightliner Terminal, Container Port.** *Peter Wilkinson.*

Top right: **Container Quay.** *Peter Wilkinson.*

Centre: **Bert Marchant with Dolly the horse.** *Courtesy of Edna De la Cour.*

Bottom left: **Holy Trinity Church.** *Rosaleen Wilkinson.*

Bottom right: **Millbrook Towers.** *Elaine Walter.*

REAR COVER

The Queen Elizabeth in the King George V Graving Dock during her refit after wartime service in August/September 1946. *Photograph courtesy of Ron Hancock, Associated British Ports, Port of Southampton.*

Foreword

This book has been published thanks to a generous gift from the Peter Barker-Mill Memorial Trust and a substantial grant from the Outer Shirley Regeneration Programme. I am very grateful to both of these organisations.

When I was asked to write this history of Millbrook, I didn't imagine it would take very long as I thought there was so little to find out. I soon discovered that I was wrong, and that apart from the old town of Southampton itself, Millbrook must have the most interesting history of any area of Southampton. From prehistoric settlements to the Second World War, there has been no era of English history which has not been reflected in Millbrook in some way. My only problem was knowing where to stop, and there remain many aspects of the area which have not been explored.

I am indebted to the staff of the Special Collections library, Alastair Arnott of the City Cultural Services, and Sheila Jemima of the Oral History Archive for their invaluable assistance. I would particularly like to thank Susan Hill and Jo Smith of the Southampton City Archives, who have been so helpful throughout this project.

I have made every effort to trace and acknowledge the copyright owners of all the illustrations used in this book. I apologise for the fact that this has not been possible in some instances.

Rosaleen Wilkinson
March 2002

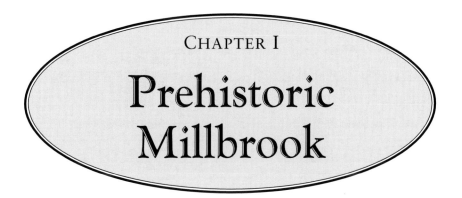

CHAPTER I
Prehistoric Millbrook

It's hard to imagine Millbrook having any history at all. To people who live in Southampton, the name Millbrook is synonymous with sprawling council housing, industrial development and an urban motorway with incessant, noisy and polluting traffic. Yet it was not always like this. People have lived in Millbrook for thousands of years, but they seem to have left little trace of their activities. Only if you explore old records and maps and history books do you discover a picture of a community stretching back into pre-history.

Imagine Millbrook 10,000 years ago, it was the end of the last Ice Age and the climate was cold and inhospitable. Britain was still joined to the Continent, and the Isle of Wight was part of the mainland. The River Test was a roaring torrent rushing down a steep valley, depositing gravels as it went. Woolly mammoth and rhinoceros, reindeer, bison and brown bears roamed the land. Several teeth of a mammoth have been found in gravel deposits locally to prove this.

Gradually the climate became warmer and as the ice receded and melted, the sea levels rose. By 6000 B.C. Britain was physically divided from the Continent and the sea had filled the Solent area, making southern Hampshire more like we know it today. The climate was still cold, however, and forests of birch and pine trees covered the land, it was too cold for oak and beech and other broad-leafed trees. In this inhospitable landscape lived the earliest inhabitants, Paleolithic hunters, people who had wandered in nomadic fashion across Europe whilst Britain was still joined to the Continent. Man has always lived in groups, and at this time small bands of people would have hunted together for reindeer, bison, bears, or birds such as geese, ducks and ptarmigan, as well as gathering whatever wild fruits, seeds and vegetation they could find in season. Somewhere with a diverse environment, between river, heath and wood, like the Millbrook area, would have been an ideal place to live. These people used tools made of stones or flints, Paleolithic means Old Stone Age. Flint tools and axes have been found

widely in the area of western Southampton, in Rosewall Road, in Millbrook Road, Emsworth Road, and in Lordswood and Rownhams.

As time went on the hunters learned to control their environment a little. By burning and felling woodland they made open glades for deer to graze where they were easier to catch. They may even have herded animals like primitive cattle with the help of domesticated wolves.[1] These Mesolithic, Middle Stone Age, hunters made small, skilfully worked flint tools called microliths, and although none have been found in Millbrook, some were discovered nearby in Rownhams. Mesolithic hunting bands probably worked individual territories most of the year but settled together during the winter.

Around 5000 B.C. climatic changes to wetter and warmer conditions and the consequent change in vegetation led to the herds of reindeer, elk, and giant red deer disappearing. In the Redbridge area, bones of huge red deer and cattle with horns six feet across, aurochs, have been found from this period. The loss of their source of food meant that the bands of hunter/gatherers had to change their nomadic lifestyle. Instead of hunting they had to adopt a more settled way of life, growing crops and herding domesticated animals to supply food for a growing population. The emergence of agriculture occurred in the Neolithic, New Stone Age, period and saw the heavily forested landscape being cleared to allow the planting of cereals such as barley, einkorn and emmer wheat. Wild pigs, cattle, horses and sheep were also being domesticated. Neolithic farmers often ruined land by their slash and burn techniques of land clearance, light soils were quickly washed away by the rain once they were stripped of vegetation and ploughed. In some areas of Lordswood and Chilworth, where the soil was light and sandy, the top-soil was eroded away and this land has been a heath with low fertility ever since.

Technology moved on slowly and by about 2000 B.C. people learned to make bronze, an alloy of copper and tin, which was useful for making tools and weapons.

These metals do not occur locally so traders must have brought copper from Ireland or Wales, and tin from Cornwall or Brittany. There are Bronze Age finds from Nursling, and a collection of pots from this period was found in Prince of Wales Avenue in Millbrook, including two which contained cremated human remains. It seems likely that land in Millbrook was used as farmland and pasture at this time.

Around 700 B.C. the Iron Age was well established and the knowledge of how to use metal was widespread. Communities were beginning to develop, land was divided up and settlements had become permanently established with systems of fields and trackways. It is in Maybush that the first real settlement in Millbrook has been found, dating from the Iron Age and inhabited between 300 B.C. and 50 B.C.

The settlement was found by archaeologists checking a building site at the corner of Romsey Road and Green Lane, ground next to Millbrook Community School farm, 'Down to Earth'. A circular trench was found, suggesting a ditch, which had been dug as a footing to hold wattle walls in place, and two post-holes in association with this, probably door posts. Several kiln structures were found, associated with layers of burnt charcoal and evidence of iron working, some hammerscale and slag. Hammerscale occurs when a blacksmith strikes red-hot iron and sparks fly up, these cool as they fall to the ground and remain shiny and uncorroded. Other burnt areas may have been cooking ovens or pottery kilns. There were nearly forty sherds of broken pottery, some of it decorated, even the remains of one large cooking pot with some burnt food still stuck on it. These pottery finds enabled the archaeologists to date the site. Various burnt stones and pebbles were found, these were 'pot boilers', used for cooking. Stones would be heated red-hot in the fire and food was placed on top of them and insulated with straw and left to roast slowly. Some flint tools were also found, scrapers and axes, no doubt people still kept things which were useful, even if they were rather out of date compared to iron tools.

Archaeologists suggest that this settlement was a farmstead where about 30 or 40 people lived, probably a large extended family group with some elderly members, younger adults, and numerous children, many of whom died in infancy. They were primarily concerned with growing food and making the necessities of life within the settlement, weaving textiles to make their clothing, making baskets, hurdles and pottery, and working metal to use on the farm as tools and ploughs. Iron ores are quite readily available in the New Forest area and the iron from worn out tools would also have been recycled.

These finds do not at first appear very exciting, but archaeology is not just about stones and bones, it aims to give substance to the people of the past, to discover them as real people. By using information gathered from many excavations it is possible for an archaeologist to build up quite a detailed picture of life in an Iron Age settlement like this one at Maybush.

An Iron Age house, evidence of which was found on the Maybush site, was circular and made entirely of timber. Thin poles were set into a ditch, about 20 centimetres apart, then wattles of hazel were woven in between them. This was then daubed with clay to keep the wind out. The only big timbers used were for the

This is what the Iron Age village at Maybush may have looked like. *Drawing by Richard Mason.*

main uprights of the door frame. The roof would be made by leaving the upright poles long and gathering them into a cone at the top, like a wigwam, and this would then be thatched with reeds. Doorways were wide and were the only source of light in the house. The doors were hurdles covered with skins, which could be slotted into place when needed. The floor was of trodden earth with the hearth in the middle, the smoke from the fire just drifted upwards and filtered out through gaps in the thatch.

Most of the raw materials needed by the Iron Age household were available locally. Wood was a vital raw material, large timbers could be cut from the dense forests in the area, and the long thin poles, which were needed for wattle and hurdle making, were obtained from coppiced hazel. Wood was the source of lighting and heating and was also the fuel for metal working. Good clay was found in the Hampshire Basin and this was used to make pottery and hearths and ovens. Although a range of farm animals was kept, the bulk of the everyday diet was based on the staple crops of Spelt wheat, barley, and Celtic beans. Spelt wheat is a hardy plant which can be winter sown, and it tolerates heavy soil like that of the Millbrook area. The fields were ploughed with a single bladed plough, an ard, probably pulled by an ox, which made a furrow but did not turn the soil like a modern one. Seed was sown by hand, and when ripe it was harvested with a hand-held sickle. Every day some of the grain would be ground up by hand on a quern stone and baked into bread in a clay oven like the one traces of which were found at Maybush.

The commonest farm animal seems to have been sheep, kept primarily for their wool. Iron Age sheep did not have wool quite like modern breeds, their coats were more hairy and had to be plucked rather than sheared. The wool could then be spun and woven into clothing. Breeds of Iron Age cattle were much smaller than modern ones and were used to pull ploughs and carts as well as for meat and leather. Pigs were useful in that they ate all manner of waste foodstuffs and quickly grew fat. Pork could be smoked or salted and kept for long periods. Unfortunately, the soil in the Maybush area is fairly acidic so any bones, which would have given archaeologists more precise information about the animals kept there, have long since dissolved away.

The earliest settlers in Maybush would certainly have chosen a site with a supply of water. As there is no stream close by, I wondered if there might have been a spring on the farm. I asked Geologist and Geotechnical Engineer, Mr Terry Rickeard, B.Sc., M.Sc., F.G.S., if this was likely. He explained that geological maps of that area show Terrace Gravels overlying layers of clay and sand. Just where the farm stood, a slight ridge in the gravel comes to an end and this would have produced a spring-line giving a constant source of water. Modern road building and drainage for housing have probably disturbed the supply of water, but it might

explain why the school boiler room periodically and inexplicably used to flood when it was built in the 1930s.

There were probably several settlements of a similar type in the Millbrook area, this was the best way of farming land which was not rich enough to support a large, concentrated community. It made better use of the land to scatter people in small groups across the landscape.

An intriguing feature of the area is the existence of several woodland rings. There is one in Aldermoor, another in Lordswood at 'Castle Hill', and in Chilworth there is 'The Ring'. These are enclosures with banks and ditches, about 50 to 60 yards across. A larger and more impressive site is at Toothill, situated in Nightingale Wood on the way to Romsey, which is a hill-top fortress. However, the origin and purpose of the woodland rings is something of a mystery. Limited excavations have failed to find evidence that people lived in them, so they do not seem simply to have been defended villages.

Several explanations of their purpose have been put forward. One explanation might be that they were constructed, perhaps as early as 4000 B.C. in the Bronze Age and that they were ritual centres, in which case the big earth walls and ditches might have been designed to look impressive. They may have been used for the excarnation of the dead. After a suitable ceremony, bodies would be placed on a platform in the sacred place and then left to rot away so that their spirits could escape back into the air. The enclosures were local centres where the community could gather to carry out rituals and make sacrifices, they were sacred places dedicated to the ancestors.[1]

Another, less dramatic, explanation for the enclosures is that they were stock pounds. Cattle and sheep would be sent out to pasture during the day, but at night they would be driven into the enclosure to keep them safe from wolves and bears. However, looking at 'Castle Hill' in the woods at Lordswood, the banks and ditches seem unnecessarily large just for keeping herds of cattle from wandering off, and it is so extensive that there would be room for hundreds of animals inside. Possibly the area was used for keeping herds over the winter and there may have been communal gatherings for feasting and the redistribution of cattle at different times of the year.

The use of the enclosures may well have changed over time. What started off as a ceremonial area may have been used later to keep cattle in, and then years later it would possibly have been seen as a suitable place to make a fortified settlement. This could have been used during troubled times, when marauding bands of raiders came to steal cattle and attack farmers. During the Iron Age, from around 600 to 100 B.C. there was a deterioration in the climate which made food production more difficult and this period coincides with the construction of many hill-forts in southern England. There may have been increased aggression and competition between communities, which resulted in raids to steal stores and cattle. The building of defended settlements reflected the need for defence and also showed off the power of the local leaders. Only extensive archaeological excavations might discover the truth about these mysterious woodland rings.

Archaeologists have been able to tell us a great deal about the way the inhabitants of the Maybush settlement lived, but the various finds do not tell us about the sort of people they were. For this we have to turn to Greek and Roman writers of the time.

The peoples of southern Britain were racially Celts, not very tall, but stockily built and sturdy. The men had clean-shaven cheeks and wore long, drooping moustaches. The people of the Hampshire area belonged to the tribe called the Atrebates, this has been established by studying the types of pottery that different tribal groups made. The Atrebates inhabited a region now roughly delineated as being between Bournemouth and Brighton along the coast, and as far north as Newbury.

The Celts were flamboyant, hot-tempered and boastful. The Greek geographer Strabo, writing between 64 B.C. to A.D. 21 described them:

"The whole race is madly fond of war, high spirited and quick to battle, but otherwise straightforward and not of evil character."

Warfare was a regular feature of life during the Iron Age. Celtic warfare often took place on a very small scale, a war might consist of just a day's fighting resulting from a raid by one tribe on another. As cattle were an important form of wealth, cattle rustling was especially frequent. The existence of the woodland fortified areas near the Maybush farm may well suggest that violence and this type of raiding were a common feature of life for the inhabitants.

According to the Roman Emperor, Julius Caesar, who mounted an invasion of Britain in 54 B.C., the Celts were a very superstitious race. The gods, in various guises, were everywhere and controlled everything. They could be propitiated by the offering of sacrifices, sometimes human sacrifices. It is possible that this type of ritual activity took place at the site in Lordswood. The heads of enemies slain in battle were cut off, embalmed in cedar oil and shown off to visitors. The Celts believed that possessing the head of an enemy allowed them to acquire his power. Offerings to the gods may have been cattle, horses or dogs, or at a more domestic level, a farmer might put some cheese or meat into a grain storage pit as a sacrifice to thank the gods for keeping the corn safe.[2]

The Celts did not have a written language so stories would be handed down from one storyteller to another. Epic tales of brave warriors, feasting, daring raids and warfare, appear in the Ulster Cycle. They are considered to be of very ancient Celtic origin and similar to the ones told in the Iron Age. I like to imagine the people of the Maybush farm sitting together by the fire in their roundhouse listening to such stories being repeated by the elders, who had heard them from the bards in their own childhood.

Rather surprisingly, the peasant farmers of southern Britain were not isolated from the wider world. Trade had taken place with communities in Europe for centuries. Whilst raw materials and luxury goods like pottery and wine were imported into Britain, many commodities for export were produced on small farms locally. Hengistbury Head, near Christchurch, was an important trading port throughout the Iron Age. The Greek writer Strabo lists the principal exports of Britain as "Grain, cattle, gold, silver and iron, also hides, and dogs which are suited to the purpose of the chase, and slaves".

From about 120–60 B.C. there was great demand from the Roman consumer market, not only for raw materials, but also for slaves. If these slaves were a marketable commodity which could be exchanged for other goods, then this would encourage powerful tribal leaders to try to obtain some. The usual way to do this was by raiding and kidnapping suitable victims. One of the explanations for the raiding and sporadic fighting which went on in southern Britain may be the slave trade.[3] When news came that an attack might be in the offing, farmers would drive their cattle to a fortified site nearby and prepare to defend themselves. If this theory is correct, it is reasonable to suppose that the people of the Maybush settlement would sometimes need to retreat to one of the nearby woodland rings. Perhaps they huddled together in the shadowy woodland enclosure at Lordswood, listening anxiously for the sound of horsemen coming to steal their animals and carry away their young men and women into slavery.

There is no evidence that the Maybush farm was inhabited beyond about 50 B.C. This may simply be because the evidence has been destroyed by farming and building over the centuries, or has yet to be discovered. Probably the land became exhausted and unproductive and the farmers moved elsewhere in the area, leaving the fields to be used as pasture or for trees and bushes to cover it again.

In 55 B.C. the Roman Emperor, Julius Caesar, brought a small army across the Channel, on a reconnaissance mission. Next year, in 54 B.C. he returned with five legions, about 25,000 men, and 2,000 cavalry soldiers. There was strong resistance from native forces, who were skilled warriors, but even so, they could not withstand the disciplined power of the Roman legions. Caesar was able to negotiate a series of treaties with tribal leaders and returned to Rome satisfied that at least a part of Britain was subservient to the Roman Empire and that trade could increase and flourish. The leaders of the Atrebates, the tribe which inhabited the area of southern Hampshire, were among those who negotiated peaceful terms with the Romans and became 'client kings'.

In A.D. 43 the Emperor Claudius launched a more

determined invasion of Britain with forty thousand legionaries. Again the king of the Atrebates, Verica, was among the tribal leaders who negotiated a peaceful settlement with the Romans. This meant that the Atrebates were spared the violence of conquest, no legionaries marched through southern Hampshire subduing the natives or destroying farmsteads. The Romans were willing to grant favours because Atrebatic territory contained good ports and harbours, such as Chichester and Clausentum (Bitterne), which could supply the legions.

When Queen Boudica (Boadicea) of the Iceni tribe, led a revolt against the Romans in A.D. 60, King Cogidubnus of the Atrebates again managed to keep his kingdom calm and avoided the dreadful slaughter and reprisals which took place in other parts of Britain. It was not until old King Cogidubnus died, in about A.D. 70 that his kingdom was finally incorporated into the Roman province and the full civil and local government systems were put in place in the southern Hampshire area.

Although the years since the coming of the Romans were years of great political upheaval, there was probably little change in the lives of ordinary countrymen. The seasons would come and go just as they always had done and the rhythm of the farming year went on. Throughout southern Hampshire there is evidence for the development of Roman farmsteads on sites previously occupied by the native people.[1] The Romans were certainly present in the Millbrook area, there was Roman pottery found at the site of Tesco's in Tebourba Way, and a Roman coin was discovered in Foundry Lane. The Romans even built a road which goes from Chandler's Ford, across Lordswood, down through Nursling, across the river and off into the New Forest. It is still partly visible in Lordswood as a wide, convex track, built up above very boggy ground. Rather disappointingly, it is not paved with stone, but is surfaced with gravel, a material easily obtained locally. Just a little way from Millbrook, however, there was a substantial Roman settlement, no doubt served by the road.

The Roman settlement at Nursling was situated where the old railway station stood. Archaeological finds at the site included stone lined wells, and the remains of a granary and a furnace. Brooches, pottery, ornaments and coins were also found. These coins dated from the periods A.D. 70–230, and A.D. 250–380. It seems certain that this was an important Roman settlement, and it is likely that farms in the locality, such as in Millbrook, would have traded with the inhabitants.

Within a generation of the Roman invasion, new ideas, new markets and improved communications were gradually bringing change and a new order to the countryside. The old hill forts like Lordswood and Toothill were abandoned and their defences neglected. They were no longer needed now that cattle raiding and tribal warfare were things of the past, and the farmers of Millbrook no doubt turned their attention to selling their goods in the villages and small towns which were beginning to develop.

REFERENCES.

1. Cunliffe, Barry: *Wessex to A.D. 1000*.
2. Cunliffe, Barry: *The Ancient Celts*.
3. Cunliffe, Barry: *Iron Age Britain*.

BIBLIOGRAPHY

Southern Rivers Paleolithic Project – Wessex Archaeology.
Crawford, O. G. S.: *A Short History of Nursling*.
'Watching brief at the site of Millbrook School', Report 246 – Southampton City Council Archaeology Unit.

MUSEUMS

The Museum of the Iron Age, Andover.

I would like to thank Dr. Andy Russel, B.A., Ph.D., M.I.F.A., who is the Archaeology Unit Manager of Southampton City Council, for his advice on this section and for showing me 'Castle Hill' in Lordswood and the Roman road nearby.

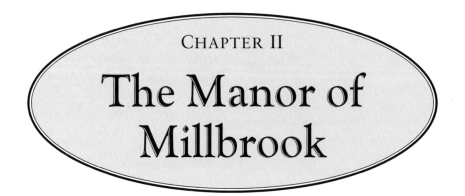

CHAPTER II
The Manor of Millbrook

The relative stability and tranquillity which the Romans had brought began to crumble as the Roman armies returned to Italy in the late 4th Century A.D. to try to save their Empire from barbarian attacks. From A.D. 367 onwards Saxon and Frankish raiders began to attack the south coast of England and the three hundred years from about A.D. 350–650 were a time of violent and rapid change. Small towns which had sprung up in Roman times, like the one at Nursling, declined as the economy collapsed. During the 5th century southern England received many Saxon immigrant settlers (from Germany) who strongly influenced and changed the native Romano-British culture. Then, in 685, King Cadwalla who was a Saxon, captured the territory of Hampshire and the Isle of Wight and established the royal family of the West Saxons as the main power in southern Britain. The region from then on can be referred to as Wessex.

Gradually a new order was established, a code of law was set up and the kingdom of Wessex began to emerge. When the Vikings attacked the area in 870 the people of Wessex, led by King Alfred, were able to resist the invaders and secure peace treaties. This meant that when Alfred died in 899 he left Wessex in a powerful position and able to enjoy a period of peace and stability.

The lands of Wessex were then divided up between the royal family, the Church and the nobility. This is probably how the system of manors developed, each one being an estate which provided an income for the owner and his family.

The nobility received gifts of land from the king. In 956 King Eadwig gave seven hides of land to his nephew Prince Wulfric. A hide was about 120 acres. The boundaries of this gift of land still delineate Millbrook, so it could be said that Millbrook was 1,045 years old in 2001.

The land charter of 956 sets out the boundaries. Some of the places are still easy to identify, but other references are open to different interpretations:

"First from Redbridge along the street to Fearninga Broc. Along the boundary to the Millbrook ford. East along the boundary to Thor's Lea, leaving it to the north. Then along the track to King's Dyke. Then along the boundary to the hollow way. To the river out as far as mid stream and along the stream bed up to the Reed Bridge."

This would suggest that the boundary ran along the road from Redbridge as far as the 'Fearninga Broc'. This is the most problematical point to identify for certain. It might mean 'the ferny brook' or it might be an actual name of a stream, 'Fearninga Brook'. It has been suggested that it was the stream which rises near the junction of Rownhams Road and Upper Brownhill Road. The stream is briefly visible near Nutfield Court, flows parallel with Kendal Avenue for part of its course, and then runs out into the Test just west of Redbridge Point.[1]

Then the boundary went along the banks of the stream to Millbrook ford, this was where the ancient trackway, which now has the modern name of Mansel Road, forded the stream. I would guess this might be near The Saints public house. Mansel Road is a continuation of Oakley Road and originally the roads formed a track from Shirley to Nursling under the name of Mousehole Lane. The boundary followed the old Mousehole Lane as far as Wimpson Lane, which was an equally ancient trackway.

The point where Wimpson Lane and Mansel Road meet is now a staggered crossroads, and this area must have been called Thor's Lea at the time the charter was drawn up.

The charter continues: "along the track to King's Dyke". This must mean that the boundary followed Wimpson Lane, crossed Romsey Road and went up Rownhams Road, turned right into Aldermoor Road, and along the track to Aldermoor Bridge, which is the probable site of King's Dyke.

From the Dyke the track continued in a fairly straight line until it met up with the 'hollow way' which led

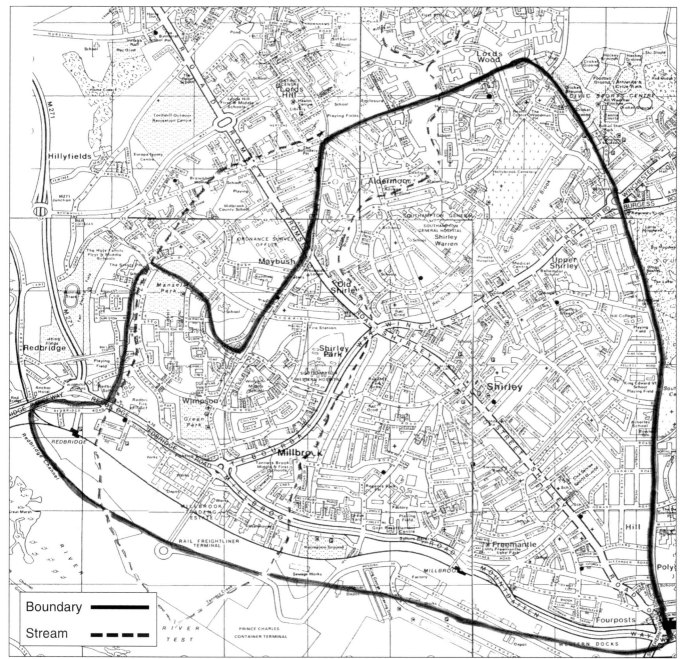

A modern street map showing the boundaries of the manor, as described in the Anglo-Saxon Charter of A.D. 956.
Reproduced by permission of Estate Publications. © Estate Publications. Crown Copyright reserved. Licence No. 100019031.

from Southampton to Chilworth. This 'hollow way' is generally accepted as being Hill Lane. The top of Hill Lane no longer continues in a straight line since the Sports Centre was built.

The last part of the boundary goes straight down Hill Lane, thus including Shirley and Freemantle, on out into the River Test and along the river-bed up to Redbridge again. The waterfront of Redbridge, with its quays, was included in Millbrook, but the bridge belonged to Nursling Manor.

The manor of Nursling abutted Millbrook, and it appears that Maybush was actually in Nursling. However, some documents in medieval times refer to Millbrook and Nursling indiscriminately so it is not always easy to be precise. It is clear that Millbrook covered a very large area, according to the Victoria

County History it was some 3,223 acres originally. In 1045 King Edward the Confessor granted this same area of land, called Melebroc, to Alwin, the Bishop of Winchester.

Some years later, after the Battle of Hastings in 1066 and the Norman Conquest, the king, William the Conqueror, "had deep speech with his counsellors and sent men all over England to each shire to find out what or how much each landholder held in land and livestock and how much it was worth." The survey was to establish the total value of land and property in the kingdom. The commissioners took evidence from the priests and reeves and inquired how many villagers lived in a settlement, whether they were free men or slaves or cottagers, how many ploughs were owned and what property existed in the way of mills or fishponds. They established what areas of land were in use as pasture or woods. The resulting information was collected into the Domesday Book in 1085. Villages were grouped into administrative districts called Hundreds, which formed regions within Shires or Counties.

The entry for Millbrook in the Domesday Book reads:

"The Bishop himself holds in the Mansbridge Hundred, Millbrook. It was always in the lands of the monastery. Before 1066 and now it answered for five hides. The villagers held and hold it. There is no hall. Land for five ploughs. Twenty-eight villagers with five ploughs. Meadow fourteen acres, woodland at five pigs. Value before 1066, later and now 100 shillings."

According to the Domesday survey the Bishop of Winchester held the manor, but the villagers claimed that it had always belonged to St. Swithun's monastery before 1066. This dispute, which also involved other manors belonging to St. Swithun's, rumbled on for many years. According to the Victoria County History, it was not until 1167 that the manor was allotted to the Prior of St. Swithun's monastery in Winchester for the support of the monks there, and this was confirmed by the Pope in 1205. However, the dispute was not settled even then. In 1284 the Prior of St. Swithun's, John of Pontissima, made an agreement with the cathedral chapter, and only then was the division of ecclesiastical estates between Bishop and Prior finally established. However, the ownership of the manor would make little difference to the lives of the villagers, they still had to work the land and pay their dues, no matter who collected the money

St. Swithun's, which belonged to the Benedictine Order, was a very wealthy monastery and owned many estates in Hampshire. The money collected from Millbrook and Nursling was allocated to the warden of works, custos operis, presumably for the upkeep of the monastic buildings. Payment in goods consisted of large numbers of pigs, sheep, cheese, butter and eggs, which were sent to the refectory of the monastery.

No lord of the manor was resident in Millbrook, so the work of the villagers would have been organised by a reeve, who was a medieval farm manager. The reeve might have been appointed by the monastery or he may have been elected by the villagers. He was sometimes an able and intelligent serf who had been given his freedom and was then promoted to this responsible position. The reeve controlled the daily work of ploughing, sowing and harvesting, and made sure that the carters, oxherds, shepherds swineherds and dairywomen did their work. He was assisted by a hayward who supervised the woods and meadowlands. The reeve was answerable to the steward of the priory. The steward was an obedientary, an official of the monastery, usually a monk, who visited the manors, kept accounts, and collected the dues on behalf of St.

Swithun's. The steward also had to hold manorial courts to settle disputes and this office was often given to prominent laymen. The St. Swithun's register records the appointment of one steward, Tristram Fauntleroy:

"Who has rendered good and faithful service in the past and is expected to do so in the future, is now named steward of all the lands belonging to the office of custos operis viz. of the villata of Nursling and Millbrok and of all lands and tenements which belong to the manor." [2]

The manor of Millbrook does not seem to have consisted of a tightly knit village with fields and woods around it. A pattern of small farms scattered at intervals was probably established in the Iron Age and seems to have survived into this period. The soil was not rich enough to support intensive arable farming so small mixed holdings made the best use of the land. Specific details of life in medieval Millbrook are sketchy, but it is reasonable to suppose that evidence from studies of manors throughout England also applied to Millbrook. In many manors the arable land was divided up into strips which belonged to either the lord or the individual villagers and the serfs were obliged to work on the lord's land for three days a week before they could attend to their own plots. No evidence of this type of field system has actually been found in Millbrook, but the land has been so heavily used and developed over time that it would be almost impossible for anything like that to have survived. It was usual for serfs to have to do any of the jobs involved in medieval agriculture, ploughing, sowing, reaping, cutting wood or hay, shearing sheep, repairing hedges or carting. In addition, at busy times of the year like harvest the whole family might be involved in boon work for the lord. Only when all these duties had been fulfilled could the serf get on with his own farm work and grow food to feed his family. The villagers also had to render payments to the lord at certain times of the year according to the customs of the manor, perhaps they had to give a goose at Christmas or some eggs at Easter.

The villagers, more correctly called villeins, were subject to various restrictions.

The villagers of Millbrook were probably serfs, since the Domesday survey does not mention any freemen. This meant that they were not allowed to leave the manor without the permission of the lord of the manor, i.e. the Prior of St. Swithun's. If they did run away they could be pursued and brought back. Without the lord's permission the serf could not sell a horse or ox, or if he did there was a fee to pay. If the serf's daughter wished to marry he had to pay a tax called merchet to the lord, and when the peasant died, the lord claimed a kind of death duty or heriot.

This all sounds very oppressive, but even though a serf could not leave a manor, he only exceptionally wanted to do so. Living on a manor provided a certain amount of security, a roof over his head and something to eat, and some serfs were given their freedom. The freeing of a serf was called manumission. An example of this is recorded in the registers of St. Swithun's in May 1442, by which time the practice had become quite common:

"Manumission granted by Prior and convent to Robert Gussyge and to Robert and John his sons, nativi, (serfs) of this manor of Millbrook. Goods and chattels as well as future offspring are included."[2]

The serf had customary rights to his house and garden, to his holding of land and to his share in the village hay harvest. In Millbrook there were fourteen acres of meadow which were specially reserved for the hay to be cut and stored as food for cattle over the winter. The serf could graze his cattle on the common pastureland of the manor and put his pigs in the woods to eat acorns, although in Millbrook there was only woodland sufficient to support five pigs. He could cut wood for repairing his house or cart, and although he was bound to work, he was also entitled to certain holy days free from labour. On these occasions the villeins would be expected to attend church. In the Domesday survey no church is mentioned at Millbrook so the villagers would have had to walk up to the church at Shirley. (This was situated at the modern crossroads of Winchester Road and Romsey Road, near The Old Thatched House pub.) By about 1280 a church, St. Nicholas', had been built near the waterfront in Millbrook. In order to support himself, the priest would have required payment of a tenth, or tithe, of everything produced on the manor.

The serf had no fear of unemployment, and, at least in prosperous times, old age and sickness were not a disaster because sons could still work the land and support aged parents. Sometimes, if people had no family they would make their land holding over to another villein in return for food and shelter in their old age. An example of this is cited in *The Five Hides of Nursling*[3]: "In 1320 John Wyeld of Wynesmannestone [Wimpson] and Aubery his wife made a quit claim agreement with Nicholas Braysfield to provide them with two quarters of flour and two quarters of barley each year for life."

By our standards, the medieval villein had a very low standard of living. The Millbrook villager of the 12th and 13th Centuries was not much better off than his Iron Age predecessors up at Maybush had been. The usual rural house consisted of a single long room with a section partitioned off at one end for a horse or cows. The house was timber framed and the walls in-filled with wattle and daub panels. The roof would have been thatched with reeds from the banks of the river Test. There would have been no chimney. Although chimneys were not uncommon in grand manor houses in the 12th century, in the peasant house, chimneys did not come in until the late 16th Century, so the smoke

from the hearth filtered out through a vent in the thatch. The diet of the villein consisted of bread and potage (a vegetable soup), eggs, some cheese, and a little meat and the occasional fish caught off Millbrook shore or in the Test.

With a poor diet and a damp, dirty home filled with smoke, the medieval peasant probably did not enjoy very good health and his livelihood was always at the mercy of the weather. From the mid 13th Century there was a deterioration in the climate, yields of corn fell and crops failed, causing food shortages. In 1338 a chronicler wrote in the account book of the Bishop of Winchester:

"From the beginning of October to the beginning of the month of December there fell such rain that the ground was rendered quite saturated and due to this there was no sowing. Then in the beginning of the month of December came a very hard frost so that the whole of the saturated ground was completely frozen and the whole earth was seen to be like ice. This frost lasted twelve weeks whence the whole of the winter sowing was as if dead, so that in March, April and May, almost nothing appeared, especially in the fruitful valleys and other good grounds."[4]

It is easy to imagine the misery and discomfort experienced by the villagers in their inadequate little houses with insufficient food and damp firewood. The ground was too hard to get on with the ploughing and the animals were rapidly eating up the stores of hay.

Yet worse was to come ten years later when the Black Death struck England. The disease first appeared in the Mediterranean region from Central Asia in 1347, it spread across Europe and is thought to have entered England through the port of Melcombe Regis in Dorset. The Black Death reached Southampton at the end of 1348. Millbrook must soon have been affected, being so near to the town and with carters carrying loads of fish and supplies into the market there every day.

The Black Death, or Bubonic Plague, has an interesting life cycle, but of course the people at that time did not understand the causes and regarded it as a visitation from God. Initially the Plague affects rats. The fleas, which live on the rats and suck their blood, carry the infection in their mouth-parts and pass it on to whatever they bite. Once all the rats have died of the disease the fleas need to move on to another host. In the medieval house, shared with cattle, there was usually a colony of rats, so fleas could easily move from the rats to the people, laying their eggs in crevices in houses. The eggs would hatch when the temperature was warm enough, which explains why the epidemic began to spread quickly in the warmth of the spring and summer of 1349.[5]

The illness starts with a fever, like influenza, and a blister forms at the site of the flea bite, rapidly turning black and gangrenous. On the second day, large painful swellings develop in the glands under the arms and in the groin, these begin to ooze pus. The vital organs are affected and fail and the skin becomes discoloured and blackened. Death results within five days in 85 per cent of cases. The disease was easily passed from person to person by way of fleas because hygiene was very poor and everyone had fleas all the time. Sometimes the Plague would cause abscesses to form in the lungs and then the infection could be spread by coughing. Death from this form of the disease, Pneumonic Plague, was even more rapid and was fatal in 99 per cent of cases.

Figures cannot be exact, but between a third and a half of the population died. Henry Knighton, an English chronicler writing shortly after the onset of the epidemic wrote,

> "Many villages and hamlets were deserted, with no home remaining in them, because everyone who had lived there was dead, and indeed many of these villages were never inhabited again. In the following winter there was such a lack of workers … that farm animals wandered about without a shepherd."

The Black Death visited England many times during the 14th Century, three episodes being particularly notable: between May and September 1349, August 1361 to May 1362, and lastly August and September 1369. No record of the effects of the Black Death in Millbrook exists, but from the Bishop of Winchester's documents it is possible to see that the epidemic certainly did hit the village.

The Plague struck the diocese of Winchester with special violence, 48 per cent of the clergy died, the highest of any diocese in England. The clergy were more exposed to infection because of their duties in administering last sacraments and conducting funerals. In 1348, an average year, 12 benefices fell vacant, but in the year of the Black Death, 1349, the Bishop had to fill 315 vacancies. John de Hegham, the Rector of Millbrook, had been given permission for leave of absence to study. He returned from his studies in the summer of 1349 whilst the outbreak was at its height and on 20 July 1349 Bishop Edington's Register records, "Church of Millbrook vacant, collation [transfer] of John de Somborne, priest, as rector." John de Somborne survived the Plague and is recorded as exchanging benefices with Robert de Mitford, vicar of the church at Britford in November 1352. In the next outbreak of the Black Death, which began in August 1361, two Millbrook priests died in quick succession. On 14 September 1361 Nicholas de Wynford was transferred to the vacant parish, and only one month later, on 19 October, the post was empty again and John Peuseys was appointed.

After the visitations of the Black Death harvests rotted in the fields and land remained untilled because there was such a shortage of labourers. Those serfs who did survive began to demand unheard of freedom from the ties of the manor and wages for their work. Lords of the manor sometimes leased their land to anyone who was prepared to take responsibility for it or else they abandoned arable farming and turned areas of land into grazing for sheep, which only required a shepherd. Whilst the manor of Millbrook remained in the hands of St. Swithun's under the direction of the reeve, it appears that the land around Wimpson was turned into a shepherdry around this time in the 14th century. The administrators of the St. Swithun's manor seem on the whole to have been fair and lenient in their dealings with the villagers. In the face of poverty and hardship they waived or reduced fees and adhered to a policy of moderation. As the number of money payments in place of services increased, so the lord of the manor assumed the status of an employer, hiring and paying wages to those who had previously done customary work.[6]

Very slowly the population began to recover and something like normal life and trade returned. The Brokage Books of Southampton record in October and November 1477 that carters, John Bryton and John Bocher, took two cartloads of olive oil, bags of almonds, a barrel of wine and sacks of cheap wool and woad for dyeing out through the Bargate to Millbrook. This suggests that weaving and dyeing of cloth was carried out in the village, probably on a small scale, and also that at least one resident was wealthy enough to afford imported wine, oil and nuts.

In 1517, Richard Fox, Bishop of Winchester, founded Corpus Christi college in Oxford and endowed it with land from various estates. One parcel of land was the field where Millbrook School now stands. It seems to have been used as grazing land for sheep and the income from it in 1534 was £1.6s.8d.[7]

Nearly two centuries were to pass after the Black Death before the ownership of Millbrook manor changed hands. Life in the quiet rural village continued as it had done for centuries before, following the rhythm of the passing seasons.

A more detailed account of life on a medieval manor can be found in *The Five Hides of Nursling* by the Lower Test Valley Archaeological Study Group.

The Mill family in Millbrook

In the 16th Century times began to change, the power and authority of the Church were questioned and wealthy secular landowners began to establish themselves.

King Henry VIII needed large amounts of money and turned his attention towards the rich estates of the monasteries. Selling off their lands and closing down the monastic communities would also have the advantage of weakening the power of the Church. In 1536 Thomas Cromwell, who was Henry's commissioner in charge of dissolving the monasteries, threatened the Prior of St. Swithun's with forced removal from office. The Prior, Henry Broke, resigned and the monastery was handed over to William Kingsmill, who paid Cromwell £500 for the favour.[8] In 1545 large areas of the monastery's land, including the manor of Millbrook, were bought by John Mill.

The Mill family originated in Sussex and in 1504 a younger son, John, came to Southampton to seek his fortune. He became involved with trade and commerce and soon grew wealthy. He was appointed Town Clerk in 1509, and Recorder in 1514. He and his son, George, also held posts as stewards of monastic lands at Beaulieu, Breamore and St.Denys Priory before the Dissolution. Like many wealthy merchants John decided to buy a country estate and in 1527 he acquired the manors of Nursling Beaufo, Swaythling and Newtonbury. During the 1540s he held important posts as paymaster for the coastal defence works and was in charge of victualling the army and fleet. With the money he was paid for this he was able to buy large amounts of monastic land in 1545, and this is how John Mill came to be lord of the manor of Millbrook.

By the 16th Century the arrangement of leasing out land to tenant farmers for a rent, a system which had begun in about 1400, had generally superseded the old manorial system. Life for the Millbrook villager went on much as before, only now he was free to leave the manor if he wished and he no longer had to do unpaid work for the lord or pay taxes for selling his horse or marrying off his daughter. The tenant farmer would pay rent to the Mill estate and he would employ labourers to do the work and pay them a wage. Of course some of the old security the serf had enjoyed had gone too, a poor labourer could no longer be sure of employment or support in old age or widowhood.

Cavaliers and Roundheads

Uneventful years passed by with their cycle of births and deaths until the troubled years of the 17th century. During the dramatic years of the English Civil War 1642–1649 the villagers of Millbrook and Redbridge found themselves in the front line of the fighting.

King Charles I came to the throne in 1625 and in the summer of that year a severe outbreak of plague hit London. The king and his parliament fled first to Oxford and then to Southampton to avoid the infection. This gave great expense to the town, a loan of £3,000 had to be made to the royal household during his stay, and the townspeople also had to endure the billeting of the king's soldiers. In 1627 the king visited Southampton again, incurring more expenditure. On this occasion he dined with Sir Charles Mill (the lord of the manor of Millbrook). Further money had to be found in 1634 when the town had to supply and equip a ship for King Charles' navy.

Despite all these expenses, it is said that the majority of the townspeople supported the king in the escalating dispute between king and parliament. However, the local Members of Parliament, George Gollop and Edward Exton for Southampton, and Sir Henry Wallop and Colonel Sir Richard Whitehead for Hampshire, were all staunch supporters of the Parliamentary cause. Then on 7 November 1642 some fighting broke out in Southampton between rival factions and Colonel Whitehead used this as an excuse to bring in troops to keep the peace. The mayor and some of the richer residents still favoured the royal cause, but fearing violence from the Roundhead troops, they agreed to submit to the authority of Parliament. ('Roundhead' was the nickname given to Parliamentary soldiers on account of their round helmets.)

Colonel Richard Whitehead was lord of the manor of Shirley and was a hard, ruthless man. He is reputed to have said, "Cruelty to Cavaliers is acceptable work to God", and he even had two Royalist prisoners starved to death at Portsmouth. As soon as Southampton was occupied he sent out orders to leading Royalists in the town, demanding large sums of money on pain of imprisonment. Sir John Mill, a Royalist and lord of the manor of Millbrook, was ordered to pay £500.

Roundhead troopers patrolled the nearby villages, arresting and interrogating people on suspicion of supporting the king. In Millbrook two Roundheads came across a farm labourer going along with a cartload of hay, carrying a large box. Suspecting that the box contained weapons being smuggled to Royalist Cavalier soldiers in Romsey, the soldiers arrested him and began a search. An account of the incident written at the time says that "armed only with a prong and a good heart" the labourer set about the troopers with his pitchfork, knocked them down, and sent them away.

This miniature insurrection made the town authorities even more nervous of a Royalist attack and the defences were further strengthened.[9]

More drama was to come the following year when on 26 December 1643, Lord Hopton sent out a troop of Cavalier soldiers from the Royalist stronghold in Winchester to break down the bridge at Redbridge. This was to prevent supplies from the New Forest reaching Southampton. A year later, in early December 1644, Royalist troops under Sir Francis Cooke were sent from Salisbury under orders to make an attack on Southampton. Coming up from the New Forest, they crossed the repaired bridge at Redbridge and were riding stealthily along Millbrook Road when they were surprised by a troop of Roundheads. A sharp battle then ensued on Millbrook Marsh. This is the area of land known as Millbrook Point where there is a sewage works. It is near the site of the old St. Nicholas' Church, so perhaps the Cavaliers were ambushed as they rode past the church and the cottages which used to stand near it. Ten of the Cavaliers were killed and the rest of the troop was put to flight, escaping into the winter mist.[10]

The Royalist threat to Southampton receded after this, but there was one more episode in the Civil War which has passed into Millbrook legend. It is said that

King Charles spent the night at Gothic Cottage, which used to stand opposite the end of Regents Park Road, near the old St. Nicholas' church.

This is the background to the legend. King Charles was imprisoned for some time at Carisbrooke Castle on the Isle of Wight and at Hurst Castle on the mainland. On either 10 or 19 December 1648, sources disagree on the date, he was escorted from his prison at Hurst Castle to begin the journey to Windsor.

The event is not well documented, but the historian G. N. Godwin, writing in 1904, claims that the route taken was from Hurst Spit to Lyndhurst, on to Ringwood, then through Romsey and up to Winchester, where King Charles spent the night. The next day the journey to Windsor continued. However, there are problems with the account. This route is very tortuous, they surely would not have gone to Ringwood from Lyndhurst before crossing the New Forest, when a shorter and more direct route existed.

It seems much more logical that the king and his guards rode through Lymington, on to Lyndhurst, across the River Test at Redbridge and then along Millbrook Road to the end of Wimpson Lane where they turned left. They would then have gone the length of the Lane until it joined the Romsey Road at the modern Maybush Corner. From Romsey they rode to Winchester where the king and his guards spent the night. The distance from Hurst Castle to Winchester is roughly 35 miles and Millbrook is at the half-way point.

In the 1930s Professor Horrocks researched documents in the British Museum to investigate the legend and came to the conclusion that it was true. Unfortunately, records say that the king spent the night at Winchester, so it seems that part of the story is incorrect, he did not sleep at Gothic Cottage.

However, the group must have stopped for rest and food and probably to change horses, so Millbrook would be a suitable point to do this. It is not known for certain what houses, cottages or inns existed in the village in the 17th Century, although claims of great age have been made for several public houses. Perhaps there were only poor farm cottages at the Wimpson Lane junction and travellers had to go to houses near the church to find refreshments and stables. Gothic Cottage may even have been a small wayside inn at that time.

A contemporary witness of the king's last journey wrote:

"Everywhere on his road a crowd of gentlemen, citizens and peasants came round him. Some were sight seekers but others prayed aloud for his liberty."

King Charles was eventually taken to London and beheaded on 30 January 1649, only a few weeks after he had sought comfort in Millbrook on his miserable winter travels.

The Great Plague

One event in the 17th Century that everyone has heard of is the Great Plague of 1665. Plague had affected England many times since the Black Death in the 14th Century, but this outbreak was particularly severe.

The first case to be reported in Southampton was on 19 June 1665. A member of the French community in the town, Monsieur De la Motte, said that the infection had been brought from London by a child who was smuggled out of the city in an attempt to save him. The boy was brought round the coast by boat and landed secretly at Millbrook and taken into Southampton to stay with a widow there. He developed the disease and the plague spread from the household.

Preventative measures against the plague included shutting up people in their homes if anyone in the household was suspected of the illness and restricting movement in and around the town. This caused great hardship and near starvation because the usual markets were closed down and food could not be obtained from local farms.

Many of the town's leaders fled, but those that remained sent out a plea for help to nearby villagers. It is said that the people of Millbrook brought food and supplies to Four Post Hill, which is at the bottom end of Hill Lane, and set up a market to provide victuals for the starving inhabitants of Southampton.

Business was transacted at a safe distance across Rolles Brook, and in order to guard against infection, the money to pay for the purchases was placed in a dish and washed in the stream before it was picked up. Fishermen from Millbrook were sent to the Isle of Wight to collect food and this was hoisted over the town walls in baskets to feed the desperate population.[11]

The register of St. Nicholas' Church, Millbrook, fortunately covers the year of the Great Plague. Surprisingly, there is no increase in the number of burials during the relevant months, the rate is constant over the years 1664, 1665 and 1666, which suggests that the village may have avoided the worst effects of the epidemic.

However, there is one grim entry which reveals that plague struck in the hamlet of Hill (this stood in the area of Hill Farm Road) which was within the ecclesiastical parish of Millbrook. Five people are recorded as dying during the outbreak, including William Wheeler and his wife, who were "buried in their own grounds, being suspected to die of plague."

Population

The population of Millbrook no doubt fluctuated over the years depending on epidemics of diseases and on the prosperity of the local economy. In the Domesday survey of 1085 there were 28 villagers recorded, but no other documents give any figures until the Hearth Tax Assessments of 1665. This tax was brought in to alleviate the financial problems of King Charles II, and created an annual levy of two shillings payable on each hearth in every house. A wealthy person would have a large house with several rooms, each heated by a hearth, and poorer citizens might only have one hearth to warm a single roomed dwelling. The very poorest people were exempt. Every house and the head of the household is listed. In Millbrook there were 65 houses, 19 of them occupied by people too poor to pay the tax. Mister Legey, with nine hearths, was the wealthiest resident, closely followed by Michael White, John Strowde, Mister Nevey and Widow Carter with six hearths apiece. Assuming that each household consti-tuted 4.5 persons, the 65 households give a population of about 293 people in Millbrook in the mid 17th century. By 1801 when more accurate counts were available, the population had risen to 1,304, fifty years later it was 6,121. The next 50 years saw the rapid expansion of Southampton and large numbers of houses being built within the boundaries of Millbrook. This took the population to 26,848 in 1901.

The original parish of Millbrook had included Freemantle and Shirley and covered 3,223 acres. Shirley became a separate ecclesiastical parish in 1836 and Freemantle followed in 1851. In 1895 both Shirley and Freemantle were incorporated into Southampton Borough and so Millbrook was reduced to 986 acres.[12]

The modern Manor of Millbrook

Over the years, the estate which John Mill had bought in 1545 was inherited by different members of the Mill family. The descent was often complicated by the failure to produce an heir and the inheritance passed indirectly through younger brothers and nephews. A biographer of the family, Tessa Lecomber, said of them:

"The name Mill is not one of those which resounds through the corridors of history, for they ventured little into the wider spheres of national, public life. They concentrated instead on what was near at hand, the affairs of town and country. All the records available reveal a family of solid, responsible landowners whose ambition comprised little more than to marry well and to add to their valuable estates."

In the 19th century, the 10th Baronet, Sir Charles Mill, left his estate to the son of his sister Mary. Her married name was Barker and her son, John, obtained a royal licence to use the surname and coat of arms of Mill, so the family name came to be Barker-Mill. In 1836 John Barker-Mill was created a baronet.

Sir John Barker-Mill was rather extravagant and spent a large amount of money on restoring Mottisfont Abbey, one of the family homes. By 1852 the finances of the estate were in such a bad way that land in Nursling and Millbrook was leased for building to accommodate the expansion of Southampton as the population increased. As the town grew steadily in the 20th Century the Barker-Mills were the prime beneficiaries. Sir John died in 1884 without an heir, and the estate was left to a distant female cousin, Marianne Vaudrey. She was "a curious and eccentric woman, dressing in her husband's old clothes". She embodied the Victorian values of piety, restraint and thrift. She handed over all the public houses on her estates to the Public Refreshment Association which sold food rather than alcohol, in the belief that drinking led to vice. In 1903 Marianne Vaudrey added Barker-Mill to her name. Marianne took seriously the traditional duties of being lady of the manor and was a benefactress to the estate. She gave generous gifts of land to the community including a church site at Maybush and twelve acres for Green Park recreation ground at Millbrook, as well as supporting the church and Sunday schools, youth and sports organisations. In 1901 Vaudrey Street in Shirley was named after her.

Marianne Barker-Mill's eccentricity and stubborn-ness affected Millbrook in a very significant way. During the early 1900s, the Ford Motor Company began to investigate various water-fronted sites in southern England with a view to erecting a large factory for the manufacture of cars and tractors. The Southampton Harbour Board favoured the scheme, so Fords purchased land at Millbrook Marsh which had a waterside frontage. During the last years of the First World War plans were made for the huge undertaking, but little publicity was given to the proposals. Then in 1922 came a serious setback. When Fords acquired the land they did not realise that fore-shore rights were involved, that the 21 acres of mud adjoining the land they had purchased was not theirs but belonged to the freeholders – the Barker-Mill Estate. The Ford Company was surprised to receive a demand from the freeholders of £200 per acre for the use of the mudlands. At first the Managing Director treated the hitch lightly, assuming that the solicitors would soon settle the matter, but Mrs Barker-Mill knew that Fords had already bought the land and made plans, so she was not prepared to reduce the price. The Mayor of Southampton, Councillor Bath, and Councillor Pugh, who was a friend of the Barker-Mill family, were asked to intervene because the scheme was so important to the economy of the town. However, if Marianne Barker-Mill was stubborn, so was Henry Ford. He refused to pay the price, whatever the result, and so Southampton lost one of the largest motor factories in Britain. Fords transferred ownership of the land to Southampton Corporation and a contagious diseases hospital and a sewage disposal works were built on the site. The Barker-Mills were left with their mud for sale and Fords went to Dagenham instead.[13]

Marianne's eldest son, Claude, was killed in the First World War. Colbury village hall was built and dedicated to Claude and to all the other men of the estate who had been killed in the conflict. When she died in 1932 the estate passed to her twenty-four year old grandson, Peter Barker-Mill.

The estate was put in the hands of new managers and they set about clearing debts by selling land and by allowing brewers to purchase all the public houses. The estate continued under careful management whilst Peter pursued an artistic career. In the 1950s a Trust was set up to take over ownership of the estate, Peter's children, Adam and Amanda, being the chief beneficiaries. Barker-Mill land lay on the outskirts of Southampton so inevitably the Corporation saw it as an obvious area for expansion. Land had already been sold off to the railways and docks companies. In 1946 the Corporation bought land in Millbrook to provide 3,217 dwellings. Then in 1964 the Lord's Hill estate was bought. This was intended to house 20,000 people, but in the end only accommodated 12,500. These developments benefited the estate, as did the Town and Country Planning Act of 1947. This Act compensated landowners for land which was scheduled as 'green belt' land and therefore lost its valuable development potential. In the 1970s the M27 and M271 motorways carved straight through Barker-Mill land, and large areas of the Millbrook estate, particularly the part close to Nursling, had to be given up to it. The Nursling Industrial Estate took 40 acres of land close to the M271.

During the 1970s Adam and Amanda began to take an active part in the running of the family lands and in 1977 the Barker-Mill Family Estate Management Co. was inaugurated. Longdown Dairy Farm was established in 1980 and opened to the public in 1985. Another commercial initiative was the Butterfly Farm which opened in 1981, this has since been sold to the Owl, Otter and Wildlife Conservancy Park.

Peter Barker-Mill died in 1994. His heirs, Adam and Amanda, both live in Hampshire, and although they both pursue independent careers in the Arts, they and their children take an active part in the administration of the family lands and play an important role in the lives of those who live and work on the Barker-Mill estates.[14]

REFERENCES

1. Burgess, Lawrence: *Streams and Watercourses of Southampton.*
2. Greatrex, J.: *Register of the Common Seal of the Priory of St. Swithum 1345–1497.*
3. *The Five Hides of Nursling.* Lower Test Valley Archaeological Study Group.
4. Titow, J.: *Evidence of Weather in the Account Rolls of the Bishops of Winchester 1209–1350.*
5. *The Plague Reconsidered.* Local Population Studies.
6. Greatrex, J.: *Some Aspects of the Monks of St. Swithuns as Landowers and Estate Managers 1380–1450.*
7. Waight, S.: *The Hampshire Lands of Corpus Christi College, Oxford.*
8. Kennedy, J.: *Laymen and Monasteries in Hampshire 1530–1558.*
9. Godwin, G. N.: *The Civil War in Hampshire.*
10. MacLachen, T.: *The Civil War in Hampshire.*
11. Sandell, Elsie: *Southampton Through the Ages.*
12. *Victoria County History.*
13. Kimber, Sir Sidney: *Thirty-eight Years of Public Life in Southampton 1910–1948.*
14. Lecomber, Tessa: *The Barker-Mill Family.*

I would like to thank Professor Colin Platt, Professor Emeritus of History, University of Southampton, for his advice on this chapter.

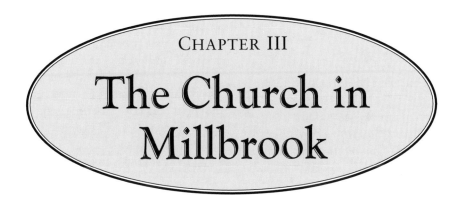

Chapter III
The Church in Millbrook

Until recent times, when secular concerns have taken precedence, the church has always been at the heart of the community, and this has certainly been the case in Millbrook over the centuries.

According to the eminent archaeologist and historian, Professor Barry Cunliffe (*Wessex to A.D. 1,000*) Christianity was established in southern Britain by the Fourth Century A.D. However, as the Roman Empire collapsed and the Romans began to leave Britain, from about A.D. 367 onwards, Saxon invaders from Germany started to arrive in the country. These new immigrants were pagan and soon swamped the beliefs of the native peoples. The re-conversion of Wessex began with the arrival of St. Birinus from Italy in A.D. 635 and his baptism of the King, Cynegils. The King's trusted nobles followed his example and over the course of time the population would in their turn accept Christian beliefs.

St.Birinus founded the first Minster at Winchester in A.D. 648 and around A.D. 670 a monastery was established somewhere in the Redbridge area. The exact site of this monastery has never been discovered and it may even have been further up-stream at Nursling. It was quite common for early monasteries to be built near rivers where goods could be transported easily. The evidence for this monastery is based on the writings of The Venerable Bede, who lived from A.D. 673–735. In his book 'The Ecclesiastical History of the English Nation' he tells the story of two young princes, brothers of Arwald, King of the Isle of Wight:

In A.D. 686 King Cadwalla, who ruled the tribes of what is now the Hampshire area, attacked the Isle of Wight and captured King Arwald. The defeated king's two young brothers escaped and fled to the mainland where they hid at a place called At-the-Stone, which was possibly Stoneham. However, they were betrayed to King Cadwalla and he ordered them to be killed. This was reported to a priest called Cynibert, "Abbot of a monastery at a place called Hreutford, which means, The Ford of Reeds", and he begged to be allowed to instruct the boys in the Christian faith

before they were put to death. This he did, and so when the young princes were executed, they met bodily death gladly.

Bede was describing the location of the monastery as being in a reedy area near a ford over the river, and this is generally taken to be in the Redbridge area. In *The Oxford Dictionary of Place Names* the derivation of Redbridge is as follows:

"The original name was Hreutford, meaning reed ford, a ford where reeds grow. The bridge built at the ford got the name Hreodbryg, which means, the bridge at the reed ford."

The monastery may have been built near the point where the original and modern bridges cross the river, but an alternative site has also been suggested. There is a field called Ruddy Mead some way above the present causeway over the River Test, which is at a point where the river divides into channels and would be easier to ford than in the area of the bridges.[1] Early monasteries were not closed communities as they became later, but their function was to teach the Christian faith to the people, and it seems likely that they ministered to the farmers of the Millbrook area. There is no further evidence about the Redbridge monastery, but it is known that an important monastery was established at Nursling by A.D. 700.

A church had certainly been built at Shirley by the time of the Norman Conquest. In the Domesday Book of 1085, which contains William the Conqueror's survey of most parts of his new kingdom, Shirley manor is described as consisting of :

"One hide land for eight ploughs, four villagers and three small-holders with two ploughs, a church, five slaves, a mill worth 30*d*, a meadow, twelve acres, woodland for six pigs, a fishery, and four dwellings in Southampton worth 40*d*. All valued at 100 shillings."

The church and main centre of Shirley manor were at the crossroads of Redbridge Hill, Romsey Road,

Winchester Road and Tebourba Way, just near the Old Thatched House Inn.

The Church of St. Nicholas

The first evidence for a church at Millbrook comes in a Deanery list of 1282 and it is probable that the original church, dedicated to St. Nicholas, the patron saint of sea-farers, had been built by this time. The Victoria County History speaks of "The plain 15th century work of the ancient tower", so the tower may have been of a later date, or there may have been rebuilding of the whole structure. St. Nicholas' Church stood more or less opposite the end of Regents Park Road at its junction with Millbrook Road. It is hard to imagine it as a church standing almost on the seashore because land reclamation has pushed the shoreline so far away now, but many of the inhabitants of Millbrook village were sailors and fishermen and the church's dedication to their patron saint was entirely appropriate.

In the Medieval period, i.e. between about 1066 and 1485, the Church played a central role in the life of the community. Attendance at services was more or less compulsory, fines could be levied if parishioners did not come to church regularly. The priest was often the only person in the village who could read, and he was a freeman, not bound to the lord of the manor like the peasants. The ceremonies and festivals of the church brought highlights into the grinding daily toil of the medieval peasant's life, and the religious teachings offered him some hope of the reward of a better life after death if he avoided sin.

There is very little information about the men who were the priests at St. Nicholas' over the centuries. Some village churches have lists of their clergy going back to the foundation of the church, but this is not the case in Millbrook, only a few names stand out here and there. In the Register of William Edington, Bishop of Winchester 1346 to 1366 there are several references to Millbrook rectors. On 24 August 1346 a dispensation was granted to John de Hegham, rector of Millbrook, of absence for study for one year at the request of Queen Philippa (wife of King Edward III), without obligation of residence. A further dispensation was granted in June 1347 and another licence to be absent for study granted on 25 September 1348. It is intriguing to wonder why the Queen should apparently take a personal interest in a priest from an obscure rural parish. Presumably the rector left a curate in charge of the parish during his absence.

The priest presided over the major events in life, the baptisms, marriages and funerals and he offered the comfort of holy sacraments at the time of death. This would sometimes put him in danger of catching diseases himself, and this happened to the priests of Millbrook during the outbreaks of the Black Death in the 14th century. In 1349 the priest, John de Hegham, perished in the epidemic. In a later outbreak in 1361

two priests, one un-named, and his successor, Nicholas de Wynford, died within a month of each other (see chapter on medieval Millbrook). After this the parish retreats once more into the obscurity of an unrecorded past for many generations.

Millbrook may have been a quiet and insignificant rural parish, but it did not escape the attentions of King Edward VI's commissioners in 1551 when the government was short of money and intent on acquiring church property:

"3rd March 1551. That forasmuche as the King's Majesty had neede presently of a masse of money, therefore commissions should be addressed into all the shires of England to take into the King's hands such church plate as remaineth, to be emploied unto his Highness' use."

The silver cross from the altar was confiscated. Fortunately for Millbrook, it was not immediately melted down, and when Queen Mary, a staunch Catholic, came to the throne in 1553, she ordered that all church property should be returned. In 1556 the cross was returned to the churchwardens.

Although the church at Shirley pre-dated St. Nicholas', gradually the church at Millbrook assumed greater importance as the one at Shirley declined. In 1574 Millbrook church became the mother church of the area as this document shows:

"1st May 1574. Robert Lanson, and William Reade, wardens of Shirley church and Radulph Matthias and William Mansbrigg, wardens of Millbrook church being present. The parish church of Shirley was in existence in far removed time as it now exists, rather small and in straitened circumstances. All tithes and rents pertaining to it do not exceed £5. The church of Shirley is becoming in a state of ruin. All the parishioners of Shirley can easily hear divine service in Millbrook. The church of Millbrook is sufficiently proper, furnished and large enough to hold all the parishioners of Millbrook and Shirley. We annexe to the possession of Richard Byrde, incumbent of Millbrook for all future time. We subject the parish church of Shirley with its cemetery to the said Millbrook church as to a mother church."
Southampton City Archives

Shirley church was eventually pulled down in 1609 and stones from it were used to enlarge St. Nicholas'.

Before 20th century land reclamation, the site of St. Nicholas' was quite close to the shore and the church always suffered from severe damp and flooding problems due to the height of the water table in that area. It was not unusual for the vestry to be a foot deep in water. In 1797 it was suggested that the church should be taken down and rebuilt, "It is a very ancient structure and in a very decayed and ruinous state and condition, and not large enough for the parishioners to assemble therein to hear divine service."

The site of the old church was to be incorporated into

St. Nicholas'
Church, Millbrook,
***circa* 1900.**
By kind permission of
Rev. William Perry.

the burial ground and the new one re-positioned slightly. Pews were to be set aside and numbered for the major households of the village. Monuments and graves were to be dismantled carefully, and no burials allowed inside the new church. During the demolition and rebuilding services were to be held at Eling.

Although an Act of Parliament was obtained to allow this, nothing was done for thirty years. On 27 January 1827 an agreement was signed between the church-wardens, John Ross of Wimpson, and John Bridger, tanner, and an architect from Chichester, George Draper. For the sum of £1,425 the church was to be altered, enlarged and completely finished to receive the congregation. Although it was not to be fully demol-ished, the plans and drawings in the City Archives show that the main body of the church was re-built and only the tower was untouched.

Despite the extensive restoration, the problems with damp could not be solved and the church continued to deteriorate. By the time Rev. A. C. Blunt became Rector in 1865, the condition of the church was causing grave anxiety, and he realised that the only solution was for a new church to be built on a new site. Immediately he ran into determined opposition from a large section of the parishioners who wanted to keep the old church as it was. At a stormy Vestry meeting in 1871, Lady Barker-Mill, the Lady of the Manor, offered a new site for the church. This offer was declined by some, but amid great uproar a poll of the parish was demanded. Bishop Wilberforce was called in to mediate in the dispute, and he came down on the side of a new church on Lady Barker-Mill's land. Vigorous opposition still continued, but in the end a compromise was reached whereby a new church would

The funeral
procession of the
Rev. Studholme
Wilson in 1907, an
important event in
the village.
Southampton
City Archives.

be built and services would also continue at St. Nicholas'. The congregation at the old church gradually dwindled away and in 1889 the Rev. Studholme Wilson, the Rev. Blunt's successor, closed the church and left it at the mercy of damp and decay.

However, the population at the eastern end of the parish was beginning to expand as housing development took place in the area. For a time the problem was solved by the erection of a temporary 'tin church' made out of corrugated iron near the railway station, but this was insufficient. The new Rector, Rev. Elton, decided that the old church needed to be re-opened. Repair work was done and in 1911 services were held once again at St. Nicholas'.

This continued throughout the First World War, but the building's useful life was coming to an end as water continued to seep into the foundations and crack the stonework.

In December 1920, the newly set up Parochial Church Council met and made an inspection of the building. They all agreed it was beyond repair and should be closed forthwith. The final service was on 27 December 1920. One week later the Rector discovered that the whole interior east wall and reredos had collapsed and crashed through the floor.

St. Nicholas' continued to stand for many years, but it was subject to constant vandalism, and eventually permission was sought from the bishop to demolish the church.

In the parish magazine for July 1939 the Rector wrote:

"The Bill for the demolition of the old church has

become an Act of Parliament. We are near the end of a problem that has weighed heavily on the parish for 150 years. It is proposed to start in August, keeping windows, buttresses, parapets and moulded stones for use in St.Clement's [a new church proposed for Regents Park Road]. The church has no architectural merit and the structure, apart from the tower, built in 1450, only dates from 1828. It has had a crisis every twenty-five years. In 1797 it was ordered to be demolished, in 1828 the nave and chancel were demolished and rebuilt, in 1870 it was condemned again and closed for worship in 1889. In 1911 re-opened after extensive repairs. The 1939 Act has been passed for its final destruction. I now have to say something terrible, and yet it must be said. The old church might have been preserved but for the conduct of the people of Southampton who have broken down every ingenuity of the Church authorities to protect it and have not scrupled even to rifle the graves of the dead."

On 8 August 1939 Southampton Corporation commenced demolition, and in less than three weeks the graveyard had been cleared and burials within the church exhumed. The bodies were reburied. Sea sand and mud filled the graves and many bodies crumbled into dust. The church was finally demolished in December that year.

The Church of the Holy Trinity

In 1871 it had been decided to go ahead with a new church on the site offered by Lady Barker-Mill at 'Bright Meadow', whilst keeping the old church open to serve the eastern end of the parish. A design for the new church in simple Early English style was approved, and the foundation stone was laid on 14 November 1872 by Mrs Vaudrey, who was heiress to the Barker-Mill estate.

The new church was finally ready for consecration by Bishop Harold Browne on Tuesday 26 May 1874. The event was regarded as a great day in the village and a charming description of the celebrations is given by the Rev. Blunt in church documents of the time:

"The whole village, from Millbrook station to the bridge at Redbridge presented a festive appearance. Flags were strung across the road at various points, and an effective arch was erected at the pond bearing the motto, 'Health and happiness to our Rector'. A most tasteful and suitable arch had been erected before the chief entrance to the church. Inside the church the floral decorations were simple but effective, those on the pulpit being especially choice. At the time appointed the Bishop arrived, and the petition for consecration was presented at the gate. The Bishop exhorted all to make proper use of the beautiful church now placed in their midst.

"It was nearly half past two o'clock before a large

Holy Trinity Church, Millbrook, photographed in 2001.
Rosaleen Wilkinson.

THE CHURCH IN MILLBROOK

The lych-gate at Millbrook Church *circa* 1914. *Southampton City Archives.*

party of about 260 persons sat down to a good luncheon in Mr Fletcher's barn. The Rector took the Chair and toasts were drunk.

"On the following day the school children were regaled with tea and cakes in the Rectory garden. In the evening 270 working men and their wives gathered in Mr Fletcher's barn. They sat down at 8 p.m. and soon the rattle and clatter of knives, forks and plates proved that full justice was being done to the various dishes, while the rattle and clatter of tongues proved that all were making themselves merry and comfortable. Cheers were given for Mr Stride, who with his great generosity supplied the beer. The party broke up exclaiming that they had never had such a party in Millbrook before."

In 1881 it was decided to proceed with the building of the tower and spire. On Saturday 13 May 1882, the Rector, the contractor and others "mounted the ladders to the summit while the choir chanted psalms. The Rector put on his surplice and proceeded to place the top stone. The choir burst out with the 100th psalm. The cross and weather vane were fixed and all descended."

There is an interesting present-day story attached to this event:

Among the possessions of the church is an ornate silver trowel, which is engraved, 'Presented to the Rev. A. C. Blunt, Rector of Millbrook, by his parishioners on the occasion of his placing the capstone to the spire of Holy Trinity Church, Millbrook, May 13th 1882'. This trowel was found in an antique shop in New Zealand, and a local priest managed to identify it as coming from the parish. In 1981, Mr and Mrs Ramson, the couple who found the trowel, visited England and came to see Holy Trinity. They

kindly gave it back to the church as being its rightful owners. Nobody has any idea how it came to be in New Zealand.

In the 19th century Millbrook was quite a wealthy parish. There were several 'big houses' in the village where well-off families lived and over the years these parishioners contributed various fittings and furnishings to the church, often as memorials. I was shown around the church by **Jim Hann**, the Churchwarden, in November 2000. Mr Hann was able to tell me a great deal about the history of the church and the Parish and

Interior of Holy Trinity Church, photographed in 2000.
Rosaleen Wilkinson.

19

I am very grateful for his help. Sadly, due to theft and vandalism, the church has to be kept locked, so it is not easy to see the lovely interior and various treasures belonging to the church. The stained glass windows are particularly beautiful. Several of the windows were given in memory of parishioners, one is dedicated to a long serving churchwarden, George Chandler, but in 2000, all these windows are covered in thick wire mesh because they have been so badly vandalised. It is intended to transfer the least damaged windows over to one side of the church and protect them more heavily, replacing them with clear glass on the other side of the building. The church is no longer in possession of the silver cross, confiscated by King Edward VI and returned by Queen Mary in 1556. The altar cross is now a brass one presented in memory of Vera McCarraher.

The oldest chalice in use is dated Easter 1913 and was presented to the church by the parish branch of the Church of England Men's Society. There are some paintings of religious subjects, which although they are old have been declared of little financial value, and near the west door, a picture presented to the church by the Royal Air Force. This is a print of a painting by Robert Taylor depicting Flight Lieutenant Nicolson winning his Victoria Cross during the Battle of Britain. He was shot down almost above the church and the picture shows an aerial view of the River Test and the countryside around Millbrook.

Other benefactors have contributed to the actual structure of the church. In 1922 the Rood screen was removed from the chancel and the McCarrahers, who acted as churchwardens over several generations, had a baldachino (a stone canopy supported on pillars) built as a family memorial. Opinions on this structure are mixed. It partly hides the east window and some people say it is magnificent, whilst others do not like it. Other parishioners contributed towards the building of a Lady Chapel in the south aisle in 1920. It is dedicated to those who died in the First World War. It has fine wood panelling and an altar furnished in scarlet cloth and decorated with a crucifix and statues of St. George and St. Michael. There is no list in the church of the names of those who died, but there is an inscription saying:

'Pray for the men of this parish who laid down their lives in the Great War, 1914–1919.'

Usually the war is considered to have ended in 1918, but although the Armistice was signed in November of that year, the war did not officially end until the signing of the Treaty of Versailles in 1919.

The names of the dead of both World Wars are commemorated in a book of Remembrance which is displayed at St. Peter's Church, Lockerley Crescent, Maybush. St. Peter's was dedicated on All Saints Day 1958 by the Right Reverend A. T. Williams, Lord Bishop of Winchester.

Those who died in The Great War are named as:

George Bowers	Albert Pentlow
Percy Bowers	Herbert Pulleyn
Charles Fisher	Herbert Southwell
Arthur Gover	Reginald Stote
Ernest Gover	William Walsh
Thomas Green	Thomas Wareham
Ernest Hillier	William Wateridge
Charles Munday	

Those who died in the Second World War are named as:

George Biddlecombe	Geoffrey Payne
Walter Brewer	Herbert Poore
Percy Bray	Leslie Puntis
William Christmas	Bertie Reeves
Thomas Churchill	John Rout
Ronald Churchill	Harry Southwell
William Egglestone	Stanley Sandy
Robert Flux	Edward Stansbridge
Frederick Grey	Richard Tapley
Harry Harris	William Tanner
William Humby	Stanley Tetley
John King	Thomas Theaker
Frederick Lane	Frank Weston
Henry Lanham	Albert Weston
James Larbalestier	Frank York

Whilst war memorials are commonly found in churches, Holy Trinity is unusual in having memorials to crew members from the parish who died in the sinking of the Titanic. Millbrook was a seafaring parish in those days and many men went to sea. The crewmen are all buried in Newfoundland, although F. H. Wormald is buried in a Jewish cemetery. E. L. Wateridge's son used to be a choirboy at the church.

'To the glory of God and in memory of the following men from this parish who lost their lives by the sinking of the S.S. *Titanic*[3] on the night of April 14th 15th 1912.

W. Bunnell, age 20	A. Curtis, age 26
W. W .Hawkesworth, age 43	A. Johnson, age 47
T. F. Pennal, age 34	B. R. Rusell, age17
F. C. Simmonds, age 25	G. F. Talbot, age 20
A.Veal, age 35	E. Ward, age 34
E. L. Wateridge, age 25	F. H. Wormald, age 46

This tablet was erected by parishioners and friends.

"And the sea gave up the dead which were in it" *Revelations*.

There is also another individual *Titanic* memorial tablet, a brass plaque inscribed:

'In loving memory of Reginald Lomond Barker who perished whilst on duty on S.S.Titanic April 15th 1912, aged 42.

Nearer my God to Thee.'

The churchyard of Holy Trinity has been in use since 1879. Some of the old gravestones were brought from St. Nicholas' and put in the churchyard at Holy Trinity, but there are no actual graves underneath them. One of these is a monument to a Scottish poet:

'The grave of Robert Pollock author of 'The course of time' this memorial poem is his monument. He was born at Muirhouse, Renfrewshire, Scotland, on the 9th October 1798, he died at Shirley Common on 17th September 1827. This obelisk was erected by some admirers of his genius in January 1831.'

Another grave was pointed out to me by Jim Hann, that of a Nelson Ward who had lived at Blighmont House:

NELSON WARD
of Blighmont in this parish
formerly Senior Chancery Registrar
of the High Court
Third son of the late Revd. Philip Ward
of Tenterden in Kent
and Horatia Nelson, his wife.
died February 6th 1917 aged 88 years

There was some speculation as to whether Mr Ward had any connection with Admiral Lord Horatio Nelson, in view of his first name and his mother's name.

I investigated the matter and discovered that Nelson Ward was indeed the grandson of Lord Nelson and Lady Hamilton. (See also the chapter on 'Millbrook Houses – Blighmont' for more information on this.)

Jim Hann remarked that:

"It is a very large building for a village church and it has hardly been altered since it was built. If someone from a hundred years ago was able to come back here they would find very little changed inside, either in the structure or the services. There's even a wire grille door still behind the south entrance doors which used to be pulled across to keep out animals when the church was left open during the day."

Perhaps one of the reasons why the church has escaped modernisation is its High Church tradition. Mr Hann explained:

"Holy Trinity is High Church, it is a long established tradition here and it just continues this way. [It appears that this High Church tradition dates from the days of Rev. Beaumont-James, 1922–1941. A faculty was obtained during his residence for Mass to be celebrated instead of Matins and for the erection of a statue of the Virgin Mary.] We use incense, the priest wears robes, and there are altar servers to offer the bread and wine at Communion, incense bearers, and acolytes to carry the candles in

The ceremony of installing a Boy Bishop at Holy Trinity in the 1960s. *Photograph courtesy of Jim Hann.*

procession. We call Communion the Mass, and the priest follows the tradition of celebrating the Mass with his back to the congregation, preserving the holy mysteries from public sight. In the 1940s, '50s and '60s we used to have twelve servers, one boy has gone on to become the Bishop of Exeter, and several others have become priests.

"We have the full ceremonies of the Church using the traditional English Missal. We used to have a choir with 30 boys, plus men, and we went in for Southampton Music Festival during the 1930s and did very well. Then there was a good sized congregation, but after the War it all changed. Nowadays it is a more working class parish. We generally get about thirty-five in the congregation most Sundays, but at Easter and Midnight Mass at Christmas the church will be packed.

"Our last Rector, Rev. Rex Holyhead, fell ill three years ago and although he was still the incumbent he was unable to fulfil his duties very often. He died in January 2000."

Since Mr Hann spoke to me, the Reverend William Perry commenced his duties as 'Priest in Charge' of the parish in 2001, and certain changes have been introduced. The use of the English Missal is to be replaced by the adoption of the new Church of England services, which were published in 2000, and Communion will be celebrated by the priest facing the congregation. This will bring the church into line with most other Anglican churches and bring the worship more up-to-date for the modern churchgoer, particularly young people. Mr Hann explained wisely, "As in everything else, we must move on to keep our faith alive."

As the population of Millbrook expanded during the 19th century and the earlier part of the 20th, it became necessary to divide the parish and new churches were built. The new parishes which emerged from Millbrook were:

St. James, Shirley	1836
Christ Church, Freemantle	1866
St. Mark's, Southampton	1892
St. Peter's, Maybush	1932
St. Jude's, Shirley Warren	1951
St. Clement's, Millbrook	1953

The establishment of St. Clement's Church was first proposed shortly after the First World War, and the church authorities hoped to buy a large house called 'Kelston' in Regents Park Road for the purpose. The house had stood empty for several years before the War, when it was taken over as a military hospital, and it was left vacant again afterwards. The Church Council negotiated the purchase of 'Kelston' and its grounds in 1924 and renovated the house to make a Parish Hall, Sunday School rooms, a Sacristy and a caretaker's flat. Then a new Rectory was built in the grounds. All this had used up the available funds and in 1935 the Rector, Father Beaumont-James, appealed

once more for financial help to build a proper church. However, the Second World War forced all such plans to be set aside and it was not until 1946 that the new Rector, Rev. R. Stephenson, was able to embark on a programme of expansion. Holy Trinity was renovated and repaired and a new church hall was built in the 1950s to replace the old tin hut behind the church. At last 'Kelston' was demolished and a small brick church built in the grounds. The little church of St. Clement's, dedicated on 9 October 1953, was only intended to be a church on a temporary basis. Once funds were available a larger building was planned and St. Clement's would become a Parish Hall, but costs have escalated and congregations have dwindled, so it looks unlikely that the scheme will ever be carried out.

In fact in 2001 it seems that the days of St. Clement's are numbered. I visited the church to have a look around. It is a very plain building, suitable for use as a church hall, with an organ, a modern font, a simple wooden pulpit and an altar on a raised dais. Unfortunately the congregation, as a record book of services shows, seldom includes more than five people, and the upkeep of the building places a strain on the resources of the parish. The Rectory, which is in the same grounds, is in a state of some dilapidation although it was only built in 1929, and would be very expensive to restore.

Proposals were put forward by the Diocesan authorities to close the church and sell the whole site for building purposes. St. Clement's ceased to be a church at a special service held in July 2001 and now awaits redevelopment.

Rectors of the Parish of the Holy and Undivided Trinity at Millbrook.

Alexander Colvin Blunt	1874–1889
Studholme Wilson	1889–1907
George Goodacre Elton	1907–1922
James Lionel Beaumont-James	1922–1941
Robert Lionel Seale	1941–1946
Ralph Westgate Stephenson	1946–1966
Leslie Richard John Moon	1966–1973
Glyn Clee Rose	1973–1980
Rex Noel Humphrey Holyhead	1980–2000
William Perry	2001

There is a Parish Prayer which was printed in a Parish magazine in 1951, it is not clear who wrote it, but most likely the Revd. Stephenson was the author.

O Lord God, our Father and Guide, be present we pray Thee, with us, to whom Thou givest in trust the welfare of this ancient and widespread parish. Prosper, we beseech Thee, with Thy blessing, our endeavour for the support and extension of Thy work, and so dispose the hearts of us Thy servants that we may render unto Thee freely and cheerfully of that which Thou hast given us. *Amen.*

Methodism in Millbrook

The Church of England was not the only denomination represented in Millbrook. An entry in the church register records the baptism of 'the child of William Pilgrim, Dissenter, 16th July 1696', and there are several other mentions of Dissenters. In 1673 the parents of Isaac Watts, who became a famous non-conformist, were married at St. Nicholas' Church in Millbrook.

Itinerant Methodist preachers would visit villages and speak at open air meetings. It is said, that in the early 1800s the first Methodist preacher to visit Redbridge took his stand under a large tree in the village but had to abandon his teaching when the Churchwardens of the parish (Millbrook parish) denounced him and his fellow preachers as "the pests of the county and the scum of the earth".[2] One solution to the lack of proper meeting houses where religious teaching could take place, was for small groups of people to gather at private houses, which were then registered as places of worship by the Methodist body. Several of these houses were set up in Millbrook: 1796 the dwelling house of Widow Collins, Four Posts Hill; 1812 the dwelling house of Mary Blandford; 1816 the house of William Morgan, registered by Alexander Weir, Minister; 1821 the house of William Allen, registered by Richard Moody; 1823 the house of Edward Tillett.

Finally, in 1859 a chapel was built at Wimpson Square. This chapel was in use for nearly a hundred years, but by 1954 it was proving inadequate and the congregation planned to build both a new church and a hall for Sunday schools and community activities. The hall was to be built first, in 1955. Congratulating the church members on their enterprise, the Mayor, Alderman Mrs V. King, said:

"Millbrook, which has only recently become part of the town, cannot be a lovely and well planned district simply through bricks and mortar. A happy community is needed too, and halls and meeting places are essential. So we are extremely appreciative that the church is stepping forward and building a hall."

The church played an important role in providing community activities on the new estate with its Sisterhood, Young Wives and Old Age Pensioners' groups. The new Methodist church in Severn Road was opened 8 May 1965.

REFERENCES

1. *The Five Hides of Nursling.* Lower Test Valley Archaeological Study Group.

2. Brown, J.: *The Story of St. Andrew's Methodist Church, Sholing.*

3. Note: There may be some confusion over the designation of the *Titanic*, whether it is S.S. or R.M.S. The explanation is as follows:
On arrival in Southampton from Belfast on 4 April 1912 the *Titanic* was designated S.S. *Titanic*. However, during her stay in Southampton, prior to her maiden voyage on 10 April, she was granted the Royal Mail Charter and became R.M.S. *Titanic*.
Information courtesy of Brian Ticehurst and Ron Hancock, Associated British Ports, Southampton.

CHAPTER IV
Millbrook Houses

The 18th and 19th centuries might be described as Millbrook's Age of Elegance. Southampton's popularity as a fashionable spa and sea-bathing resort began in the 1750s, and this provided the stimulus that led to the setting out of large estates and the building of many fine houses. Millbrook, with its charming waterside situation, pretty countryside and nearness to Southampton was an ideal place for this type of development.

One of the earliest houses to be built was Shirley House, which stood somewhere in the Clarendon and Henty Road area. It was built around 1760, probably for Richard Wilson, who owned a plantation in the West Indies. In 1792 it was sold by auction. The particulars gave a glowing description:

"A spacious elegant new-built freehold house with double coach house and stabling for eight horses. Excellent kitchen gardens, surrounded with lofty walls, a pleasure ground disposed with great taste. A beautiful paddock of about thirty acres, a small farm house, barn, granary, dove cote and rich meadows, making about forty-eight acres."

The house was bought by Mr William Fulke Greville and he owned it from 1792 to 1802. Not a great deal is known about this gentleman, but he was related to the Earls of Warwick. In *The Hampshire Chronicle* of 5 September 1801 it was announced that Mrs Greville, wife of W. F. Greville of Shirley House, had died aged 36, and that she was buried at Owslebury church. A month later the paper contained an advertisement for the auction sale of the contents of Shirley House.

"Capital household furniture, including 2 piano-fortes, and other valuable effects of a gentleman quitting his residence."

A drawing from Louisa Rich's sketch book 1819. It shows St. Nicholas' Church and cottages in the village, as viewed from the grounds of Shirley House. Boats on the River Test can be seen in the distance. *Southampton City Archives.*

The house was bought by the Rev. Sir Charles Rich, and he lived there until his death in 1824. So that his southerly views would be preserved, Sir Charles leased 34 acres of land in the Oakley Road/Waterhouse Lane area from the lord of the manor, Sir Charles Mill.

As befitted his calling as a clergyman, Rev. Sir Charles Rich involved himself in Millbrook parish affairs. He and Lady Rich gave gifts of money towards the purchase of blankets and flannel for the poor at Christmas and Sir Charles headed the Vestry Committee which, in 1816, was considering the addition of a schoolroom to the Poor House at Wimpson. His daughter, Louisa Rich, no doubt led the sheltered and leisured life of young ladies of the time, spending her days practising her music, sewing, and painting the charming countryside in which she lived. A collection of her drawings is preserved in the Southampton City Archives and they show a view of a picturesque and tranquil Millbrook.

After Rev. Sir Charles Rich died in 1824, his widow remained there until 1833, and then the estate was sold to a local business syndicate which included William Henry Roe. He became sole owner in 1853. During the 1840s the house was leased by Major General Sleigh and then it became vacant in 1852 and Mr Roe advertised the estate for sale or rent. The house itself was let, with twelve acres of land, to Rev. H. N. Burrows who ran a private school until 1859. Other parts of the estate were sold to Mr Sampson Payne as building plots and by the 1860s they were built up with villas and cottages.

A caretaker, John Webb, lived at the mansion between 1862–70 keeping the house and kitchen garden in good order, but after he left, the building remained empty and began to deteriorate. It was reputed to be haunted by the ghost of a young woman whose death was connected with her parents' efforts to prevent her eloping with a stable lad, and indeed the caretaker's son had found the skeleton of a small baby hidden in the attic. Perhaps its haunted reputation put prospective tenants off, but it was never lived in again and was demolished in about 1886.[1]

Another fine house of this era was Blighmont, an eight bedroom mansion set in an estate of 50 acres to the west of Waterhouse Lane. It was built in the early 1800s by Admiral Sir Richard Bligh, who was distantly

The advertisement for sale of Shirley House in 1852. *Roe Album, Southampton City Archives.*

related to William Bligh of the mutiny on the *Bounty* fame. He had the house built for his son, Captain George Bligh, who had been severely wounded at the battle of Trafalgar, where he served as Nelson's flag lieutenant on the Victory. In about 1835 Captain Bligh moved to Hythe, leaving Blighmont to be occupied by Nathaniel Jeffries, who had previously lived at Hollybrook House. A gentleman called Adam Atkinson lived there for a time, but then in 1852 the Naghten family moved in. Arthur Naghten was an M.P. and County Magistrate and the ladies of the family are frequently mentioned as visitors to Millbrook School, taking a charitable interest in the villagers and their children. Arthur died in 1881.

By a strange twist of fate the house's connection with British naval history was repeated when from 1900–1918 Blighmont was occupied by Nelson Ward, who was the grandson of Admiral Lord Nelson. The inscription on Nelson Ward's grave in the cemetery of Holy Trinity Church states that he was the son of Philip Ward and Horatia Nelson of Tenterden in Kent. Horatia was the illegitimate daughter of Lord Nelson and Lady Emma Hamilton, born in 1801. Although Horatia never acknowledged that Emma was her mother, she was very proud of her relationship to Lord Nelson and named her son after him. Horatia had married Rev.Philip Ward in 1822 and after his death went to live with her son Nelson in Pinner. She died in 1880. Nelson Ward lived at Blighmont from 1900 until his death in 1917.

By 1921 Blighmont had become a nursing home, which functioned until 1963 when British American Tobacco bought the house and demolished it.

Freemantle Park probably started life as a farmhouse, it is mentioned as far back as the 14th century. It was acquired about 1775 by James Amyatt, who enlarged and improved it into a fine Georgian mansion. Amyatt was M.P. for Southampton from 1784 to 1807. James Amyatt had made his fortune as a merchant in the East India Company and he must have brought home a native servant to Freemantle. In the Parish Register of baptisms it is recorded that on 27 December 1774, George Freemantle, black servant of James Amyatt Esq. was baptised. This must have caused quite a sensation in the village at the time. In 1790 he moved into a smaller house near Millbrook, which was described by a Guide Book of the time as "a pleasant village with several genteel houses extending nearly to Redbridge."

Freemantle Park was then bought by John Jarrett who spent a great deal of money having the interior made, according to Baker's guidebook of 1804, 'sumptuously elegant' being inlaid with Italian marble.

After Jarrett's death in 1809 there were other short term occupiers and then in 1822 it was bought by General Sir George Hewett. He had made his career in the army and had served as commander-in-chief in India 1807–11, being created a baronet in 1818. He was apparently a well-respected gentleman, being involved in the administration of the Poor House in Millbrook for several years. He died in 1840 and in 1841 Lady and the Misses Hewett presented communion flagons and plates to the parish church in his memory. The family continued to own Freemantle Park until 1852 when the estate was sold for building land and the house demolished.

Lordswood may seem very far removed from present day Millbrook, but in fact land there belonged to the manor of Millbrook and the Barker-Mill family owned Lordswood House. Lordswood, simply meaning 'the wood belonging to the lord of the manor' was the name of woodland which extended from Aldermoor to Chilworth. Lordshill was a dead-end road which sloped steeply down from old Rownhams Lane to Tanners Brook. This was situated between the old Bedwell Arms pub and Aldermoor Road. There were about six houses in this steep lane and water often ran down the hill from various springs. It was locally known as 'soapsuds alley' because several washerwomen lived in the cottages and threw out their soapy water into the lane where it mingled with the spring water into a foaming stream.[2]

Lordswood House may have originated as a 19th Century hunting lodge. It had always belonged to the Barker-Mill family and fireplaces in the house were thought to have come from Mottisfont Abbey, which the family also owned. It was bought by General Sir Neville Chamberlain in the 1870s and fancifully extended in the style of a Swiss chalet. Sir Neville retired to live at the house in 1881, he and his wife sharing it with his sister and brother. After Sir Neville died in 1902, his widow continued to live there until 1920. A lady called Blanche Needham then took it over and made it into a hotel and later a riding school. The house stood between Abbotsfield Close and Grafton Gardens, it was demolished in 1972.

Aldermoor also seems a long way from Millbrook, but this area too was owned by the lords of the manor. Aldermoor House was built around 1800. The house and its sixty acre estate always belonged to the Mill family who let it out to tenants. The farm buildings were located some distance from the house to avoid farmyard smells and noises annoying the residents, and these still survive on the south side of Aldermoor Road. In 1932 the Barker-Mill family sold the whole estate to Southampton Corporation for immediate housing development and the big house was demolished.

Crabwood House at Maybush still survives. It was built in the 1840s, probably for Francis Marrett, owner of a shipyard in Southampton. Various tenants leased the house over the years, little of interest being known about them, and the house was last used as a private residence by a Mrs Tudway 1927–1938. In 1936 the property was sold to Claremont Estate Company, but two years later, before they had started

Blighmont House in the 1940s. *Southampton City Archives.*

Regents Park, an engraving by Philip Brannon, 1850. *Southampton City Archives.*

work on development, the Ordnance Survey bought Crabwood House and its surrounding land. Crabwood is currently the Ordnance Survey social club.

There were a number of 'genteel residences' in Millbrook village and Regents Park Road, which were mostly built in the early Victorian period from about 1840 onwards. The name 'Regents Park' gave an air of elegance and refinement to the area. The artist Philip Brannon published a guide book in the 1850s describing its situation as 'admirable, the aspect warm, the surrounding country varied and rural and the prospect extensive and full of interest.' Regents Park Road itself

was said to be a 'gracefully winding road' which was lined with 'handsome suburban residences' set in extensive grounds. The road had wrought iron gates at each end, which gave the impression of a private estate.

The names of some of the houses, which have nearly all been demolished over the years, are commemorated by road names, Clifton, Claremont and Lansdowne. A large property called Kelston stood on the site of St.Clement's church. During the First World War it was used as a military hospital, in common with many large houses, and locals spoke of seeing lorry loads of coffins being delivered there. In 1924 it was converted inside

The carriage gates and lodge at the Shirley end of Regents Park Road in the early 1900s. *Photograph by F. G. O. Stuart.*

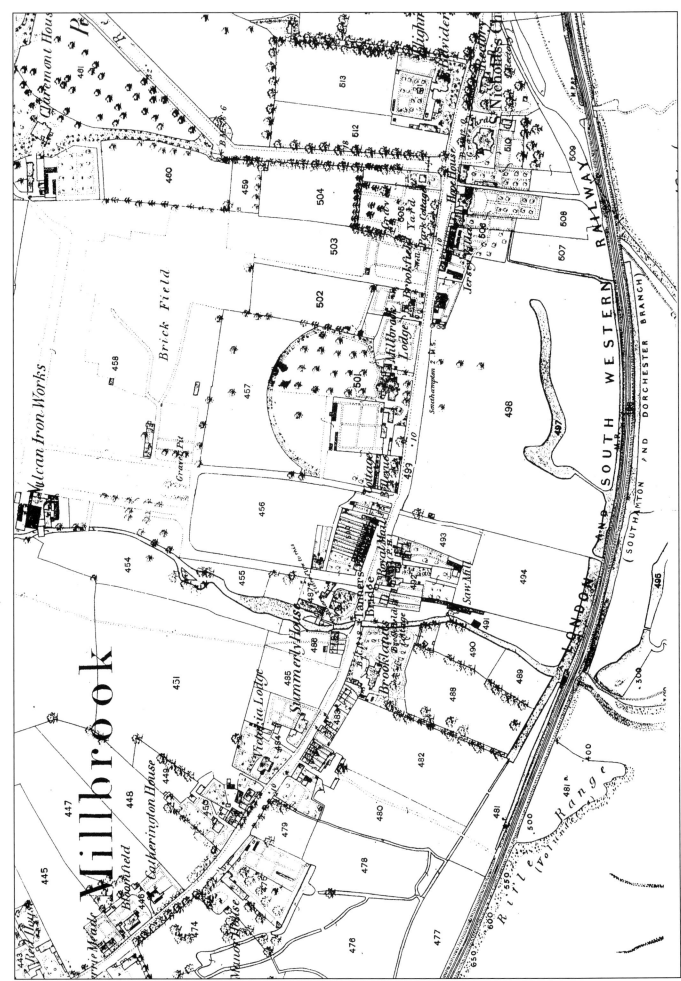

A map dating from 1867 showing some of the large houses in Millbrook village. *Crown copyright.*

THE MILLBROOK NURSING HOME,

PHONE
2400.

Medical, Surgical, and Maternity.   *120 Foundry Lane, Southampton.*

for use by Millbrook parishioners and re-named Church House. Once sufficient money had been raised, St. Clement's was built in the grounds and the house was demolished in 1952.

The last remaining elegant house in Millbrook village is Baronald, which has bow fronted windows overlooking the speeding traffic of Millbrook Road. It was built around 1900, replacing a house called Belvedere Villa which dated from 1868. It was the home of Brigadier W. W. Thornton, whose son, an army captain, was killed in the First World War. During the Second World War it was requisitioned by the army and an extension was built at the back for use as a cookhouse. At some point during the war it was used as a Home Guard post. More recently it has been converted into flats.

The Victorian residences such as Bloomfield House, Summerly House, Victoria Lodge, Catherington and Elmleigh House were all demolished when road building commenced after the war. It seems a pity that the road could not have been aligned a hundred yards or so nearer the waterfront so that the village did not need to be destroyed.

REFERENCES
1. Leonard, A. G. K.: *More Stories of Southampton Streets.*
2. Sibley, B. and S.: *Past Glimpses of Nursling and Rownhams.*

BIBLIOGRAPHY
Vale, Jessica: *The Lost Houses of Southampton.*

Elmleigh House, which stood next to Holy Trinity Church. *Photograph courtesy of Jim Hann.*

The Millbrook Poor House

There have always been poor people in society, people who have struggled to find shelter and enough to eat, but the problem of pauperism, or the absolute depths of poverty, did not really arise in the Middle Ages. The standard of living for the majority of the population was very low, but the insecurity and uncertainties, which beset the working classes in later years, were not such a problem. Whilst bad weather and the failure of the harvest might mean near starvation for the people who lived on a manor such as in Millbrook, there was no fear of unemployment or homelessness. Everyone on the manor worked together to grow food and to provide services for the village, such as that of the miller or blacksmith. When someone became too old to work, they could rely on their family to take over their land and provide for them. If they had no children, arrangements would be made with another villager to take on their holding in return for food and necessities. (See Chapter II – The Manor of Millbrook.) Monasteries also provided help for the sick and needy.

However, after the Black Death, the manorial system went into decline and people began to work for a wage. Life became less secure, workers could lose their jobs and probably the home that went with it. In addition to this, King Henry VIII closed down most of the monasteries and convents after 1536 and this left destitute people with nowhere to seek help.

The secular authorities had to fill this gap, and the Beggar's Act of 1536 placed the care of the poor on parishes. The underpinning feature of the provision was settlement in your own parish, so villagers were very wary of strangers coming into their community. Newcomers had to prove that they were renting a home or had some means of support, and that their own parish would have them back if they fell on hard times.

Pregnant unmarried women were hastily moved on out of the parish because an illegitimate child would become an expense on the parishioners. Orphaned or destitute children were found apprenticeships so that they were cared for and trained at no expense to the parish. In the 16th and 17th centuries the poor were thought of as the lower orders of society and the provision of assistance for them was aimed at suppressing vagrancy and crime. The able-bodied were expected to find employment and charity was reserved for the deserving poor.

Until the mid 18th Century the usual way of assisting the destitute was to give them a sum of money to help them to survive in the village, but in 1782 parishes were enabled to join together and form a Board of Guardians to oversee the care of the poor. In 1816 a committee of the leading parishioners of Millbrook, led by Sir Charles Rich, agreed to lease land from Sir Charles Mill to build a Poor House. It was proposed that a house for 20 persons should be erected along with 10 or 12 small cottages to accommodate another 40 poor residents. This stood in the area of the Bricklayers' Arms public house at Wimpson.

Mr Hobbs tendered for the building work and the new Poor House opened its doors on 21 June 1819, the rooms having been warmed by the best coals, the yard gravelled and the bedding inspected. Charles Pearce and his wife were appointed Master and Matron at an annual salary of £20, and Mr Caldwell was employed as parish surgeon, apothecary and man-midwife to care for the inmates. His duties also included attending the parish lunatics at Grove Place, as listed in the records for 1836. The paupers were subject to strict rules and regulations. They had to worship at church on Sundays, the gates of the House were to be locked at 9 p.m. and not opened after that hour upon any consideration. The residents had to clean their windows every month and sweep in front of their doors every day. The Poor House privy was to be cleaned each Saturday. Children had to attend the parish school, which was set up in a room specially built at the Poor House. Girls were taught needlework and boys some useful occupation, and all were to be apprenticed outside the parish when they were 'of an age'. In 1822 a further schoolroom, the Parochial

School, was erected in the grounds for the children of the labouring poor of the parish (i.e. for children who were not resident in the Poor House).

Local farmers and traders supplied the Poor house: J. Giles supplied bacon, J. Horton sent groceries, J. Parsons provided butter and C. M. Wheeler delivered the coal. However, it is not recorded who tendered successfully for the two gallons of gin per week which were doled out to the residents!

In 1820 the problem of poverty in the area was so considerable that the Parish Council decided to take advantage of an Act of Parliament which allowed the establishment of 'Select Vestries' to oversee the care of the poor. The committee, under the chairmanship of Sir Charles Rich, kept tight control over expenditure so that money was only spent on those who deserved it. In August 1821, William Stride was brought before the magistrates for refusing to take employment on a ship and leaving his wife and family dependent on the parish. He was later supplied with a jacket and trousers to the value of 20 shillings to enable him to go to sea. In 1822 Anna Philpott had to swear on oath who was the father of her unborn child so that he could be made to support her, otherwise an illegitimate child had to be taken into the Poor House at parish expense.

The parish also employed destitute labourers to do work around the village such as road mending and ditch clearing, but complaints were made that they were not doing a fair days work and the Overseer was instructed to check that they were coming to work before 7 a.m. and not leaving until 5 p.m. In 1825 an official was appointed to "follow all beggars and wandering persons out

A notice dating from 1830, informing parishioners about new regulations for the relief of the poor. *Southampton City Archives.*

of the parish, a coat, staff and hat to be provided to the purpose." People who were not originally from the parish were sent back home if they required relief. In April 1835 Henry Bale was to be properly clothed and sent to Manchester by the wagon to his sister Mary, who promised to provide for her brother if the parish would pay the expenses of the journey.

The poor could also turn to private charities for help. In Millbrook the Rev. William Harvest had left £100 in his will in 1815 to provide blankets to be given to poor families having the greatest number of children under eight years old. Susannah Pollen left a bequest of £333 in 1822 for blankets and warm clothing to be distributed at the discretion of the vicar. Money was also given by Sir Charles and Lady Rich, Sir George Hewett and H. Barlow (Gent).

Goods were purchased in advance, the accounts for 1824 list 6 cloaks at 8/–, 123 yards of cotton at 7d, 140 yards of flannel at 10*d* a yard, 5 blankets at 10/9, 6 rugs at 5/6.

The charity was distributed at Christmastime each year and poor families came from miles around to receive gifts; villages mentioned in the records include Cocks Ford, May Bush, Aldermoor, Lordswood, Wimpson and Redbridge. The gifts received are also listed in detail, such as the cloak given to Wm. Goffe of Shirley Mill, "the cloak of former years being moth eaten", and George Noyce's daughter receiving three yards of calico and a gown on going into service. Shirts, cloaks, gowns, stockings, counterpaines (bedspreads) and blankets were given out, as well as material such as calico, gingham, flannel and fustian, for making clothes.

The reasons for the person qualifying for help were also written down, "old", "crippled", "widow", but amidst all this generosity there was no compassion for anyone who had brought troubles upon themselves. In the list for Christmas 1824 there appears the entry; "Hannah Broomfield – an illegitimate child, refused".

The popularity of the charitable gifts eventually exceeded the money available for providing them, and in 1855 the Rector, J. Haldane Stewart discontinued the distribution, saying, "It was found that the practice created in the minds of the poor an erroneous impression as to the actual annual amount of the two charities". By this time, Shirley had been divided from Millbrook as a separate parish and as a result the clergy and wardens demanded their share of the charities. Of the £6 left in the Pollen Charity fund, Millbrook took £4 for flannel and blankets and Shirley had £2.

More positive measures to help the poor were made in 1831 when four acres of land at Pickles Copse were set aside to be cultivated by unemployed agricultural labourers "on their own account", rent free. (Pickles Copse once stood on the site of Newlands School, and a few large trees remain in the playing field.) In 1832 the committee decided that it was desirable to encourage emigration to the British colonies "as a means of relieving the parish of those persons who are usually a burden on the parish in the winter months". In February 1834, John Dolan, his wife and five children were granted £12 towards the expenses of emigrating to America.

The administration of the Poor Relief did not always run smoothly. In 1828 William Budd of Botley was appointed assistant Overseer for the parish, "to act in all cases of bastardy, to apprentice poor children, and inform himself minutely as to the circumstances and character of all persons claiming relief", and to collect the Poor Rates from householders in the parish. However, when the accounts were examined in October 1832 a large debt of £400 was found, and further investigations revealed that Mr Budd had collected money but not recorded it in the rate books. He was immediately dismissed and attempts were made to recover the money, but they were too late, he

had already absconded with £226 of parish money. Although £5 was advanced to the High Constable of Southampton to apprehend him, he was never found and the Poor Rate was increased to pay off the debts. The next Master and Matron of the Poor House had to give a £200 surety for the faithful discharge of their duties.

The Poor Law Act of 1834 enabled parishes in an area to group together in a Union to provide relief for the poor, and in May 1835 the Vestry held a meeting to discuss the possible union of Millbrook with Chilworth and North and South Stoneham. It was resolved to resist this because it was a severe reflection on the rate-payers to presume that they were incompetent to manage their own affairs. Secondly, "the removal of the aged and afflicted inmates of the Poor House to a great distance from their relatives and connections will prevent many kind friends from sympathising in their misfortunes by little attentions and additions to their comfort, the absence of which will materially embitter their days". The South Stoneham Poor House was at West End, now known as Moorgreen Hospital, and this was a long way from Millbrook in days when journeys were made on foot or by horse and cart.

The Poor Law commissioners rejected the plea and on 2 June 1836 the inmates residing in the Poor House were ordered out within a week. Arrangements were made for the disposal of the Poor House and it was auctioned at The Ship Inn at Redbridge on 25 October 1837. The House and grounds were bought by Henry Kernot, but it is not clear what happened to the buildings. In the Tithe map of 1840 it is listed as being occupied by the labourers of William Sharland who owned the tannery next to Tanners Brook. Beyond that date I have not come across any firm information about its use, although some of the buildings may have been used as classrooms for the old Millbrook School.

No further mention is made of the residents turned out of the Poor House; it must be assumed they were sent to West End.

In more recent times several other charities were set up. The Ross Charity dates from 1901, £16 was available annually to provide coal, blankets and clothing for 32 parishioners. The Sarah Spinks Charity too was established in 1901 and was also known as the Millbrook Flannel Charity as it supplied material for warm underclothing. The Prior Charity gave money for groceries at about the same period. These charities, along with the remaining funds in the Pollen and Harvest Charities, were all united in 1930 and administered by the churchwardens. The newly formed Millbrook United Charity paid £25 for the services of a Queen Victoria's Jubilee nurse to tend the sick in the parish. In 1948 the grant was given to the Southampton Nursing Association. By the 1950s the fund was administered by trustees led by the solicitor, David McCarraher, and gave specific gifts of up to £5 to help with sickness, old age or widowhood and indentures for apprenticeships. Most recently, donations have been made to charitable bodies such as the Association for the Blind and other welfare organisations, but the amount of money is very small and these gifts have not been made in the last ten years.

No account of charity in Millbrook should leave out the Thorner's Homes in Regents Park Road. The Homes originated in a bequest made in 1690 by Robert Thorner of North Baddesley. He wished that almshouses should be built in Southampton for the support of poor widows, and eventually this was done in 1793. The almshouses were situated at the Marlands, and when the Southampton Town Council decided to build the new Civic Centre on the site, the residents were forced to move out. In 1929 the trustees bought a large house, Clifton Lodge, and two acres of ground in Regents Park Road. Blocks of flats were built and the residents moved in gradually, the whole estate being fully occupied by 1932. The gardener lived in Clifton Cottage. In 1937 the trustees bought a further plot of land in Clifton Road, this included the dilapidated Clarendon Lodge, which was demolished. More flats were built on this site in 1971 and the development was called West Court. In 1986, a house adjoining the Homes, 135 Regents Park Road, was bought for use as a common room for the residents, with a flat for the warden on the upper floor. As living standards improved, the Homes began to seem out of date, so in 1987 a major restoration and refurbishment programme was begun. In 1993 Thorner's Homes celebrated their bi-centenary.

BIBLIOGRAPHY

– all in Southampton City Archives.

Millbrook Parish Select Vestry, D / Z 327 / 2

Millbrook United Charities, D / CCI / 66

Harvest and Pollen Charities, D / CCI / 6

Rose, A. and Hunt, B.: History of Thorner's Homes 1793–1997.

CHAPTER VI

Millbrook School

The first school in Millbrook was opened in June 1819. A committee of local dignitaries, led by Sir Charles Rich of Shirley House, was considering plans for a new Poor House in 1816 and it was suggested that a schoolroom for a parochial school should be built alongside. Sir Charles Mill, the Lord of the Manor, offered two acres of land for the site of the Poor House just off the modern Wimpson Lane, near the Bricklayers' Arms public house. The children who lived in the Poor House or who were dependent on parish charity were to attend this school. The girls were to go in the mornings and the boys in the afternoon. Girls were to be taught needlework and boys trained in some useful occupation, and all were to be apprenticed "when of an age" outside the parish. The Poor House and parochial school opened in 1819.

Then in November 1822 it was suggested that part of the garden of the Poor House should be used for the erection of a schoolroom for the children of the labouring poor of the parish, that is, those who were poor but had employment. On 7 October 1824, Thomas Benham, a local builder, submitted his estimate for building two schools, a dwelling house and two privies, for the sum of £325. "The whole of the works to be executed in a good, substantial, and workmanlike manner". The estimate was accepted and the work was to be completed by 1 July 1825.

Unfortunately, no records exist for the early years of the school, but in 1862 the keeping of a Log Book became compulsory and Headteachers were required to keep a diary of the day to day activities of the school. The Millbrook Log Books date from 1 March 1863. They make fascinating reading and create a vivid picture of school life from Victorian times to the present day. It is interesting to compare them with the Log Books of Foundry Lane School, which was also within the boundaries of Millbrook. In their day to day concerns, the two schools reflect their surroundings. Millbrook School had attendance problems caused by children doing agricultural work instead of going to school, and in the early years, many Foundry Lane children suffered the distress of urban poverty caused by overcrowding and unemployment.

March 10th 1863

The school, after a breakfast, dismissed to keep the marriage of H.R.H. the Prince of Wales with Princess Alexandra of Denmark, as a holiday.

March 31st 1863

Several of the most promising boys just upon leaving for brick making for the summer. This is one of the difficulties in connection with progress in this school.

May 15th 1863

My daily experience in school teaching on this place is certainly not encouraging, what with my pupils being irregular in attendance, the offspring of illiterate parents and naturally most unintellectual, results are slow in presenting themselves.

July 31st 1863

School dismissed for four weeks, Harvest Vacation.

September 8th 1863

Several boys away in potato fields where the crops are now gathering. There is little doubt but that irregular attendance is the greatest check to progress in schoolwork. I know of no remedy for it, as it arises from the extreme poverty of the parents, who are in consequence of that poverty glad to turn the usefulness of their children to some account, either directly by sending them into the fields, or indirectly by placing them in charge at home while they go out to labour.

School attendance was always a problem because education was not compulsory and child labour was commonly used in agricultural areas like Millbrook. In 1873 the Agricultural Children's Act raised the minimum age at which children could be employed in farming to 10 years, but it was difficult to enforce. It was not until the Education Act of 1880 that schooling up to the age of 10 was made compulsory.

September 12th 1864

Numbers thin, children absent gathering blackberries, and others in picking acorns. Friday is always the worst day for attendance in the week and it is difficult to alter it, the parents not caring enough for their children's education to admit of a stringent rule.

HER MAJESTY'S INSPECTOR'S REPORT 1863

BOYS The school is doing very well. The attainments of the boys are creditable but the school is not so quiet or the discipline so precise as might be desired.

GIRLS The school is likely to do well under existing arrangements.

The annual examination, usually held in November, and the Inspector's Report on the results, were a source of much anxiety to both pupils and teachers in Victorian times. The Inspection determined the grant paid to the school according to the success of the children in the examination. Each child had to pass in three subjects, reading, writing and arithmetic, to qualify for the full grant of 8 shillings (40p) per child, 2s 8d (13p) being paid for each pass. The success of the school could be measured by comparing the number of children entered to the number of actual passes.

In the 1863 Inspection at Millbrook School 40 boys were entered for the examination, so there could be 40 x 3 = 120 passes, the result was 94 passes. In the same examination 24 girls took the tests and achieved 62 passes out of a possible 72. The Infants were not tested, the grant being awarded on attendance figures, in 1863 there were 21 pupils under six years old at 6s 6d (32p) per head. The total grant awarded in 1863 was £34.11.0.

Pupils were also tested on their singing and recitation of poems by heart. Lists of songs and poems appear in the Log Books every autumn term. These had to be learned throughout the coming year ready for the examination.

April 10th 1864

Some of the boys leaving for the summer. These lads find employment in the brickyards of the neighbourhood from April to October and return to school with little of the former winter's work in them. This commences about the age of eight and continues up to school leaving age about twelve. Many children unable to attend school from the poverty of their parents owing to the general depression of all kinds of work.

In 1867 the employment of children under the age of seven was prohibited.

May 29th 1868

Charge of the school relinquished after been held for eleven years and six weeks.

J. E. Duncan.

Note by Managers
Mr Duncan resigned in consequence of reducing the salary, he leaves carrying with him our respect and good wishes. He has gone to Highfield. Mr Charles Carter from Warminster is his successor.

June 23rd 1868

Opened school, children somewhat unruly. Master had a deal of trouble today. Teaching was out of the question, whistling and singing were prevalent to the detriment of discipline.

July 24th 1868

I think the children's general behaviour is better both in and out of the school than when I took them in hand. I observe a great disinclination to work by themselves, they waste time talking and playing and say they cannot do the arithmetic. They will not exert themselves.

June 1st 1869

Several children absent. One child has been absent ten weeks from having no shoes. Two other children in the same class are now entirely absent to nurse the babies while their mothers are out washing [*i.e. their mothers were washerwomen*].

August 3rd 1869

A drenching morning, only 38 children present. Robert Hurst and Charles Cooper absent from having no boots.

June 19th 1870

Ellen Mintrim has left this week to go out to service. She is only ten and is very backward indeed.

May 17th 1872

Exercise books have been introduced for entering sums, after being worked upon slates and passed by the Master. I have difficulty in getting many children to try the manuscript books instead of their slates.

July 26th 1872

On Wednesday a great many boys were away looking at a cricket match. I cautioned the Pupil Teacher about coming late and other little things such as faults of discipline in class. This led to an interview with his mother to whom the Master gave a full account of his shortcomings.

The use of Monitors and Pupil Teachers in Victorian schools was an economical way of assisting the Master or Mistress and also training future teachers. Monitors were bright senior pupils who were given the task of teaching children in lower Standards than themselves. They might be as young as thirteen and not much older than their charges. Monitors were paid a small wage and sometimes went on to become Pupil Teachers. These would serve a four or five year apprenticeship and could then go to a Teacher Training College to become Certificated Teachers.

The contracts and indentures of several Millbrook Pupil Teachers are in the Southampton City Archives. Martha King was engaged as Pupil Teacher on 1 November 1864 for five years until 31 October 1869. Her wages were £2 quarterly in the first year, to be increased by 10s (50p) per quarter in each subsequent year of the engagement, but this would be stopped if she failed an examination. The Pupil Teacher was to have five hours instruction per week after school from the Certificated Teacher and could be dismissed for idleness, disobedience or immoral conduct. Needlework was an important subject for the female teachers and Pupil Teachers were marked separately for each skill in hemming, gathering, run and fell seams, button holes, frills, tucking, patching, darning, gussets, coral stitch and also knitting

The unsatisfactory male Pupil Teacher mentioned by the Master was Edward Harrison who lived in Shirley. His contract was from 1870 to 1875, but he resigned on 24 December 1874 saying that he wished to follow another profession and never having given entire satisfaction to either the Managers or Master of the school.

February 28th 1873

Through bad attendance, caused partly by the neglect of parents and partly by bad weather, we cannot seem to make progress. With teachers' love, zeal and earnestness being treated with such indifference, it is no wonder they often feel depressed and disheartened. I, as Master of this school feel the depression.

August 2nd 1873

On Thursday afternoon the annual Treat took place at the Rectory grounds, the weather being all that could be desired.

January 21st 1876

The Committee has made the school mixed and the girls are to be transferred to the schoolroom and taught with the boys. In the afternoons they leave the schoolroom after the first lesson to have sewing. The girls at present do not seem so sharp as the boys, they are very dull and inactive.

December 8th 1876

Kate Roud, the Pupil Teacher should endeavour to exercise more control over the children, especially the boys. I have told her that discipline must be obtained. Many of the boys are very rough and require a strong arm to rule them.

June 8th 1877

The attendance of the children now begins to flag. Many children to field work. When there is no employment in the shape of scaring birds, weeding or hay-making, the children are sent to school and in winter the schoolroom is crowded to excess.

September 28th 1877

The Education Act [*of 1876*] is driving into school those who have never attended school at all, or if so, very little. Their attainments need not be stated. The children seem to have forgotten a very great deal during the Harvest Holiday.

November 1st 1878

Had rehearsal of songs on Wednesday afternoon. Mrs Shores and Miss Fletcher of The Red House attended and expressed themselves highly delighted with the singing.

Songs for the examination:-

Summer song	Brave comrades	Laughing morn
Men of Harlech	Rule Britannia	Evening lullaby

November 15th 1878

The annual examination took place. It commenced at 10 a.m. and was conducted by L.W. Green Esq. The singing went off nicely. Over eighty children were present.

Attendance of visitors good at examination, the Rector and his Curate, the Rev. Buttermer, C. Dayman Esq. (the village doctor) and Mrs Charles Dayman (of Victoria Lodge), Mr Hall (from the Manor House), the Misses Naghten (of Blighmont House), Miss Wroe and Miss Buttermer.

The local gentry, particularly the ladies, often involved themselves in the village school. Sometimes they would call in with guests and expected to hear the children sing or recite for them, or they would look at the needlework. Many of the gentry gave donations to the school, so perhaps they felt entitled to do this. Other ladies and gentlemen, although totally unqualified, often took over classes on a regular basis, teaching reading or scripture or sewing. It must have been difficult and disruptive for the school teachers.

September 10th 1880

Measles have unfortunately made their appearance in this parish, consequently many children have not attended.

The Education Act of 1880 made school attendance compulsory and school Attendance Officers were employed to try to enforce this, with variable success.

January 21st 1881

Weather very stormy, rain and sleet fell and the wind blew with a fury. During the night snow fell heavily and in the morning the roads were impassable. School closed.

October 28th 1881

Several children play truant. The irregular attendance of the boys is to be regretted, as the girls come so much more regularly there is a great difference in the respective quality of their work. The school Attendance Officer said that he cannot help it. He was not properly supported by the Magistrates and he was powerless to act. He was so much disheartened that he intended at Christmas to resign.

October 16th 1883

Sent expressly for many absent children. Various excuses, "no boots", "minding the baby", "has to go somewhere" were the most common.

HER MAJESTY'S INSPECTOR'S REPORT 1884

Allowance is made for the changes in the teaching staff, several of whom have resigned this year, but this is not sufficient to account for the remarkably unsatisfactory condition of the school. Organisation is bad and discipline is by no means well maintained. The children are not taught habits of cleanliness and neatness. Writing and arithmetic are bad, English singularly defective. Standard III could not be more backward. Unless improvement is generally effected a serious reduction of grant will next year be incurred.

January 5th 1885

Opened school today with boys only. Girls have been under the Master's charge since 1876. Girls are now instructed in the other department.

Mr Charles Carter gave up the Headmastership of Millbrook National Boys' School on December 31st 1885 after having occupied that position for ten years. He was succeeded by Mr Robert Bollom.

Arithmetic to be taught for the Examination in each Standard.

St. II   Multiplication,

St. III   Long division,

St. IV   Multiplication and reduction of money

St. V   Fractions and proportion

St. VI   Vulgar fractions

St. VII   Averages, percentages, weight and longitude.

April 24th 1888

Military drill is to be taken from 4 o'clock to 4.30 p.m. [*This is the first mention of any kind of physical education for the children*].

April 1st 1889

After morning school the Master missed a shilling [5p] from the school money. A boy named Charles Dorey confessed he had stolen it. Mr Dorey came in the afternoon and thrashed his son before the boys in the school. [*In 1886 the Attendance Officer had discovered that Dorey, then aged eleven, was not at school because he was working as an errand boy.*]

November 20th 1890

Sent Henry Batten home owing to the dirty and disgraceful state of his dress.

Sent Collins home on account of hairworm.

January 19th 1891

School fees to be raised to *3d* [1.5p] per week for the oldest child and *2d* [1.25p] for the remainder. There are to be free dinners for poor children.

Free education was inaugurated on 31 August 1891, and the school leaving age was raised to eleven in 1893.

May 30th 1894

Dr. Pern, the Medical Officer of Health gave instructions that the water in the school well should not be used for drinking purposes. Cardboard modelling and coloured crayon drawing introduced from the 1894 Code of Suitable Occupations.

An example taken from an examination card of about 1890. A child of twelve would have been expected to do this calculation. Can you?

December 14th 1894

Scheme for horticulture approved. Boys take gardening from 2.30 to 3.35 p.m. on Fridays. Received schedule from Her Majesty's Inspector for gardening.

Proposed syllabus of lessons to be taken in horticulture.

St.I   Object lessons in the violet, primrose, daisy, potato, turnip, cabbage, raspberry, plum, apple, fork, spade, watering pot.

St. II and III   Seeds and their requirements, nature and composition of soils.

St. IV and V   Nature and function of roots, stems, leaves and branches.

October 10th 1898

List of children defective in one or more particular.

Weak intellect	8	Medically unfit	7
Defective eyesight	3	Deaf	2
Speech impairment	2	Idiot	1
Displaced hip	1		

There was no special provision for handicapped children.

July 18th 1900

School closed for village flower show. Children secured 10 out of 15 prizes offered in the competitions, and 11 extra prizes for excellence in garden work.

July 20th 1900

St. I visited the village pond and noted many forms of pond life. [*The pond is now the site of Millbrook Roundabout.*] St. III visited the neighbouring woods and collected grasses and wild flowers.

The general effect of Cottage Gardening on the children is very beneficial. The faculties of observation are strengthened, memory is aided and judgement formed. Ideas of care are instilled and a feeling of responsibility is generated. It arouses the interest of the parents, there is better attendance and increased interest in other lessons.

February 1st 1901

School closed on account of the funeral of Her Late Majesty Queen Victoria. A memorial service was held in school at 9a.m.

September 12th 1905

Miss Crabbe started Domestic Economy with the girls when the boys are at gardening.

May 2nd 1908

Empire Day. The children paraded in front of the school at 3 p.m., the Union Jack was raised and saluted, God Save the King and various patriotic songs were sung.

May 7th 1910

King Edward VII died today.

June 16th 1911

Closed school for a special week's holiday in honour of the Coronation of King George V.

The First World War broke out on 4 August 1914. Thousands of young men immediately volunteered to fight, and there must have been hundreds of Millbrook boys among them. Foundry Lane School records over three hundred of its past pupils on active service in 1915, but the Millbrook Log Books make little mention of the War.

May 24th 1917

Empire Day. The Rector addressed the children on frugality in the avoidance of the waste of bread during the national crisis.

November 11th 1918

Victory announced this morning. Owing to the closing of the various workshops, many children absent in the afternoon.

March 3rd 1919

Much sickness in the parish, twenty deaths in one week owing to the prevalence of influenza.

December 10th 1936

King Edward VIII abdicates, the Duke of York acceded to the throne as King George VI.

December 22nd 1936

Mr Davis, Headmaster, retired today.

January 4th 1937

I, Wilfred Henry Mitchell, have taken over the headship, 141 children on the books. I have noted the dilapidated condition of the buildings and outside offices.

Mr Mitchell left on 31 January 1938 and was succeeded by Mr E. Brown.

The old Wimpson Lane school was by this time inadequate for the needs of the modern curriculum, having no facilities beyond the basic classrooms and outside toilets. The rooms were still heated by open coal fires, which smoked profusely, and the new Headmaster complained that the children were cold and uncomfortable. The Millbrook Parish Magazine, October 1935, announced that the Wimpson school was to be closed and the County Authority proposed to erect four new council schools for boys and girls, both senior and junior, in the Maybush area. Nearly three years later the old school was finally closed. On the last day the Rector explained to the children that the church had done all it could for them, Millbrook always having been a Church School, and now the responsibility passed into other hands. The Rector blessed the children, "and so, not without a tear, all was over."

April 13th 1938

The Rector spoke to the whole school, telling the children its history and wishing teachers and children every good wish. After prayers and the singing of "O God our help in ages past," Mr Ransom, a Manager, gave the final word of dismissal and the Rector shook hands with every child. It was a sad farewell to all around. The school has been a bad building with excellent teachers, and upon teachers, schools depend.

The Parish Magazine reported on the opening of the new school in Green Lane.

"On Wednesday April 27th 1938 the new Council Senior School was opened at Maybush. All children of the district above eleven years will attend here in the future. The external appearance of the school is pleasing and solid. A wholly new concept of education comes into operation. A child goes to a junior school up to its eleventh birthday and after that to a senior school with improved methods of instruction, designed to give every child in the land something of the advantages gained by secondary school education. Mr W. L. Mackay has been appointed Headmaster."

The school opened with 367 children on the registers. The addresses of the children give some indication of the still rural character of Millbrook. Among the homes in ordinary streets like Kennedy Road and Ashby Road, there are many country addresses, Upper Wimpson Farm, Pondside Farm, Bridger's Farm, Bargain Farm. Horticulture was a well established subject on the curriculum at the old Wimpson Lane school. In the 1930s it was still a village school, and for many of the pupils learning about scientific horticulture and gardening was very relevant to their home-life and even to their future employment.

Gardening was on the syllabus at many schools in Victorian times, but as more and more people went to live and work in towns it became irrelevant and the subject was dropped, Foundry Lane School discontinued gardening classes under instruction from the Local Education Authority in 1924. Millbrook School was fortunate in having an enthusiastic teacher in Mr Weston who was keen to continue the gardening tradition, and the spacious grounds to allow it. Almost the first entries in the new Log Book are:

May 11th 1938
Requisitioned gardening tools.

July 5th 1939
Mr Weston absent attending a course in Gardening and Rural Science at University College, Southampton.

The new school had only been open for eighteen months when war was declared on 3 September 1939. Unlike many Southampton schools, Millbrook was not evacuated. It was considered to be in a safe country area, and in fact children from Portsmouth, Gosport and Ilford in Essex were evacuated to the school. Sadly, the area did not prove to be a safe haven for two evacuees from Portsmouth. The Log Book records that Ada Burley, who had been living at Fernyhurst, in Rownhams, was killed by enemy action on 26 June 1940, and Dorothy Ward, staying in Lower Toothill, was killed 20 July 1941. Both girls were victims of bombers indiscriminately dumping their loads after an incomplete raid on Southampton.

Peter Lisle, who lives in Redbridge, wrote down these memories of his schooldays at Millbrook during the war years:

"I was born in Redbridge, in Oakridge Road, in 1929. My two sisters, Barbara and Sheila were also born there. It used to be called Oak Road then, but when Redbridge was taken into Southampton in 1954 it was changed to Oakridge because they already had an Oak Road in the town. I went to the old Redbridge Infant School, the red-brick building on Millbrook Road. At nine years old I was transferred to the Green Lane School. At about this time

the old Millbrook School at Wimpson was still in use, but eventually everyone was transferred to Green Lane. The old school at Wimpson was about 100 yards from the corner of Mansel Road and the Bricklayers Arms pub. In that 100 yards were two rows of small cottages called Nelson Place and Wellington Place and a Methodist chapel. Behind the school was a small farm run by a man called Sid Southwell. His brother Andrew had a farm at Millbrook Pond.

"During the war years the old school was used as an A.R.P. post. My father was a Special Constable before, during, and for a time afterwards. At some time they must have put in a billiard table, because I can remember that some evenings he took me there to show me how to play snooker, it must have been about 1943/4. After the War it was used by a motor repair firm for repairs, paint spraying and body work. Once the new council estate started being built they moved to new premises and the old school was pulled down.

"When we were first transferred to the new school at Green Lane a bus was run to take us from Redbridge to school, but when the war started the bus service was stopped and we had to walk. Half the walk was on farm tracks and if it rained it got a bit muddy. I went through Wimpson Farm, across Mansel Road and into Green Lane, which really was a lane at that time. It did not worry us that we had to walk; there was no other way we could get to school. Once we had passed Green Park there was only the farm and about two houses, compared to today it could be called isolated. There was no shelter, if it rained you got wet. In winter it could be almost dark when you left for school and dark when you got home. At Wimpson Farm there was a pond and in winter, if it was frozen over, we would stop and slide on it for half an hour on our way home. They started running the bus again towards the end of the war.

"We had the best of both worlds. There was the big town of Southampton handy, but we considered we were living in a village, with countryside and space around us. At school age we were allowed to play outside until approximately 8 o'clock in the evenings and then we had to be indoors. In wintertime we stayed indoors, played cards, read a book, did jigsaws or listened to the radio. There was no television then. In summer we had the space to roam. Lots of time was spent on the old bridge and the shore, fishing when the tide was right, and a lot of swimming. We used to use the old bridge as a diving board.

"I suppose you could say the war years were exciting for us, there was lots of activity, not always good. We got used to air raids and took them in our stride. There were one or two times when the raid was heavy and got too close, then perhaps I got a bit nervy, especially at night. It isn't until years later that you think about it and you realise the best thing was getting out of your shelter and still being in one piece. At the age of eleven or twelve you can't see the dangers. We used to watch Spitfires and German planes fight overhead. I remember a pilot called Nicolson, the only V.C. of the Battle of Britain, coming down by parachute and landing in the field opposite the old Redbridge School. Another pilot baled out at the same time, but he was not so lucky. His parachute collapsed and he spiraled to the ground quickly and landed somewhere near Clifton Road in Regents Park. On one occasion, I was standing on the corner of Allington Road, talking to one of my closest friends, Bill Lewis. We had been fishing or swimming on the bridges most of the afternoon. My mother had come to the end of the cutway by our house, shouting at us as loud as she could to come home. We didn't take a lot of notice until she pointed to the sky and there was a large formation of German bombers coming our way. That made us move and get into the shelter!

"There are so many memories. We might have been up half the night with all the noise from the raids, but next morning everyone went to work and we went to school. We may have been tired at times, but I can't remember ever being stopped from going to school. Everything carried on as usual.

"We would collect pieces of shell shrapnel and maybe a bit of a plane, even once a 'live' incendiary bomb. They were small and light, about 15 inches in height, I managed to find one in a ploughed field on the way home from school. My father was always on at me because I would pick up anything that looked interesting. Being on the outskirts of the town, we were involved with raids but a little detached from the main targets. Most of the bombs fell on the town, but there were many that fell outside the town. We seemed to spend hours in the air raid shelters. One of the worst raids was on 30 November 1940. It started at 6 o'clock in the evening and went on until 2.30 in the morning. When we came out of the shelter, I looked towards the town, the sky was red, a lot of the town was on fire. There was plenty of activity at the time before the D-Day landings and afterwards. Green Park was an American Transit camp at that time and it was covered with tents.

At the Green Lane school we had an air raid shelter for all the classes, we seemed to spend most afternoons in the summer of 1940 in them. They were in the playing field, near Romsey Road.

As we got older, thirteen or fourteen, we used to have gardening and woodwork one afternoon a week. The gardening teacher was Mr Harper, if I remember rightly. He came from Portrush in Northern Ireland, everybody liked him. We did not have animals, or our own plots, just larger plots to attend to. On your afternoon you did whatever needed to be done. We went through the whole process, dug the ground, planted seeds, hoed it and watered it. Vegetables were grown, I can't remember

ever growing flowers. Anything from the garden went to the kitchen for school dinners. The meals were fairly good considering how things were at that time, and you never got chips with everything like you do today. For a time the school meals were stopped and we had to take sandwiches. If it poured with rain on your half-day, Mr Harper would take us to a classroom and talk about things to do with gardening. Nobody took any exams or got any certificates and I can't remember any one of us going to work in agriculture, although some had come from a farming background. I have a fairly small garden and still like digging and planting seeds and seeing them grow. Maybe it comes from my schooldays. Lots of people had allotment gardens to grow vegetables for their families. My father had one and after tea in the growing season I would often have to spend an hour weeding carrots, parsnips or anything else that needed weeding before going out to play. I left school in 1945."

From the time the new school opened in 1938 until September 1955 when Mansel Road Infants was built, Millbrook School catered for all age groups. In 1955 all the Infants transferred and the school became a Secondary Modern Mixed. In 1960 new premises were built and the school was divided into Millbrook Boys and Millbrook Girls, then in 1967 the two schools amalgamated once more to become Millbrook School, a neighbourhood, co-educational, comprehensive school. Today, pupils transfer to Millbrook Community School from Shirley Warren Primary, and from Fairisle, Newlands and Mansel Junior schools.

In the 1960 brochure for the Girls' School, which is in the Sandell Collection in the City Archives, the headmistress, Miss Thorne, said that the new school offered an education for the differing needs of girls in the neighbourhood. The motto 'Veritas' – 'Truth', was chosen to inspire the spirit of loyalty and sound purpose on which the tradition of the school would be founded. The curriculum was to develop a sound character through the integrity and happiness of each girl. The subjects offered were: Art, domestic science, English, French, geography, history, mathematics, music, needlework, religious instruction, physical education and science. There was a school flat to train girls in housecraft. The uniform was a dark green skirt with a white blouse, tie, green cardigan, blazer, and a felt hat. Green gingham dresses were worn in the summer and green knickers and white plimsolls were required for games. A satchel for books was desirable. The school was officially opened by Lady Pamela Hicks on 8 December 1960.

A Gardening and Science annexe had been erected in 1957, and once the girls had moved out to their new accommodation, the boys were able to occupy this fully and new facilities for woodwork, metalwork and technical drawing were built.

I spoke to two ex-pupils of Millbrook Girls' School

who were there in the 1960s, Eileen Downes and Maureen Harvey.

"When the Girls' School was in Lower Brownhill Road and the Boys' School was over in Green Lane, we were separated, we could only look at the boys and they could only look at us. There was an invisible line, which ran across the school field, and woe betide anyone who crossed it! We started at the school in September 1964 and there was a new headmistress, Miss Wood."

Eileen Downes – "We had to wear gabardine mack-intoshes in the winter, and some girls wore berets. If you were a prefect you had a red or green tassel on your beret. My mother bought me a gabardine when I was eleven, which would have fitted Arnold Schwarzenegger. She hoped that it would last me my time at the school. I used to try and lose it, but I never succeeded. In needlework we had to make ourselves a school summer skirt, either cherry red or apple green. It was yards and yards of material held up with elastic, you could have used it for a sail on a yacht, but everyone had the same so we didn't care."

Maureen Harvey – "We had assembly every day, it was very traditional with hymns and prayers, and sometimes after assembly there would be checks on your fingernails and on the length of your skirt. Short skirts weren't allowed, they had to cover your knees, but as soon as we got outside the school gate we'd roll the waistband over to make a mini-skirt."

Eileen – "The only time we could wear trousers was if it was very cold, and then you had to change back into a skirt when you arrived at school.

"Most of our teachers were spinsters and they were very ladylike and genteel, they didn't shout. When the first three years became mixed in 1967, it was a real shock to see how some of the masters treated the boys, we couldn't believe it. Eventually the whole school became mixed sex classes, though I was not in one or taught by a male teacher. We used to get 'debits' for bad work or talking in class and you were so ashamed if you got one, but the boys got slippered or caned across the fingers or backside depending on the misdemeanour."

Maureen – "We were pretty well behaved, we had to be. If you were sent to the headmistress that was really terrible, you weren't smacked or anything, but just the look on her face and the tone of her voice was enough. There was a bench outside her office door and if you passed anyone sitting and waiting you really felt sorry for them.

"We had Domestic Science and there was a school flat which we had to run as you would a proper house. You see, we were expected to leave school, get a job for a few years and then get married and be a housewife, so we had to know how to do things the right way. The flat had a kitchen, a bedroom and a sitting room.

Eileen – You were taught how to make a bed properly, how to lay a table with all the right cutlery, and even how to wash up, doing the glasses and knives and forks first.

Maureen – "We used to serve afternoon tea, and when we got higher up the school we could plan a menu, cook the meal, and invite one of the teachers to lunch in the flat. We learned polishing and cleaning too, that flat was spotless. So if you weren't shown these things at home, you learned at school.

"I left school at fifteen before I took my G.C.E.s, my Dad said I could leave if I got a job, so I took the first thing that came along, working in a shop, C&A. We were pigeonholed really, we knew our place. If you were very bright you went to work at the Ordnance Survey and if you had no expectations at all you went to work in the tobacco factory."

Eileen – "I was in the 'middle' so I went into office work, shorthand and typing, and I went into the Gas Board. Our mothers used to take part of our wages towards the housekeeping, there was no negotiating how much, she decided, and that was that. In our day nobody from here went to university, it wasn't expected of you. We were expected to get a job, meet someone, and get married and have children quite young."

Maureen – "When I took the 11+ exam I passed to go to the Girls Grammar School, but I didn't want to go there and wear all that stupid uniform, I flatly refused. Several girls and boys from my class at junior school did go on to grammar schools and you can see now what a difference it made to their lives, they got the good jobs and more money. But people who went to Millbrook School have done really well for themselves too."

Eileen – "I passed my 11 plus as well and obtained seven C.S.E.s in my fifth year. All in all my school days were very happy and I enjoyed my time as a librarian and prefect."

I spoke to two teachers who taught at the school in the 1980s, Carol Duce and Barbara Hayes. It's interesting to see school life from a teacher's point of view, rather than how it seemed to the pupils.

Carol Duce and Barbara Hayes – "We taught at Millbrook in the 1980s, and it was a jolly good school. The Headmaster in the late '80s was Mr Lowry and he was very accessible both to teachers and pupils. Miss Tosdevine, 'Tossy' as we called her, was the Deputy Head, she was an amazing woman, and there were five or six others who were the real backbone of the school. There was Don Cartridge, Ken Oliver, John Mason the Art teacher, Dave Pedder, he did music, and Colin Jones. Together they made up a really strong group. They had been there for years and years and they knew the school and they knew the sort of kids we had, and they knew how to cope with them. Some of them had been teaching there twenty years or more, since before the school became co-educational. They gave the school stability. Then they all got to retirement age at more or less the same time and left the school.

Barbara Hayes – "What I found hardest to fight against was the low aspirations of both the children and the parents. It was very difficult trying to persuade a kid to stay on into Sixth Form education, or even to achieve much in their G.C.E. exams. Some of them used to go on to Sixth Form College all full of enthusiasm, and then you would get a report six months later and half of them had left. Most parents expected the children to go out and get a job, not to continue their education.

"Most of the parents were pleased to be living in Millbrook. Previously they may have worked in the docks and lived in the old part of the town, Northam or St. Mary's, but now they had moved out into the suburbs on to what was, in theory, a nice new estate. It was out of town, there was a lot of greenery around, and the houses themselves were nice. There was nothing for the kids to do though, I don't remember any youth clubs, there was nothing else to do but hang around the streets.

"I always liked teaching the boys, they never bore you any grudges, you could run them up hill and down dale and afterwards they'd just say, quite cheerfully, 'All right then, Miss!'

"Girls are different, they'll remember it ten years later. School is quite different today, there is all this emphasis on achieving exam passes and the old traditional skills have gone out of fashion."

Carol Duce – "I taught Domestic Science and I loved it at the school. Mrs Morffew took over in 1988, after Mr Lowry, and she was Head for three years. She was keen on the Cookery side of things, but when she left it coincided with the time when they were trying to cut Domestic Science out of schools altogether. Cookery would no longer exist, and the manual skills like woodwork and metalwork were being dumped as well. All of a sudden we were doing Food Technology and the kids were designing pizzas on a piece of paper, not actually making them. I had children in the group who could barely read, let alone work out calorific values.

"When I first taught at Millbrook we had real cookery. We did theory, everything about the nutrients in meat and fish, milk and eggs and vegetables. That was followed up by a practical demonstration and then the children did it themselves. We'd make puddings like apple crumble, and scones and fairy cakes. The older classes would cook complete meals, perhaps in pairs, one did the main course and their partner made the pudding. If children enjoy a subject and are interested in it, they're keen to learn and they don't make nuisances of themselves. We had boys doing it as well, some of them preferred it to woodwork or metalwork. The idea of it being a subject that girls needed to do in order to equip them for

looking after the home had died long ago."

Barbara – "It was a shame, because practical skills are the one thing that people really need. One teacher, Nick Fielder, used to take the most difficult boys who were nearly at school leaving age and teach them car maintenance and other skills, like D.I.Y., things that were really relevant.

"I didn't really have discipline problems, but you always had to work at it. You had to impress them that you knew what you were doing, if they sensed a chink in your armour they were straight in there. Parents' Evenings were very successful, the parents would collect the child's report at the door and then be able to go and talk to the teachers about it. The parents were very much 'on our side', but education wasn't their priority."

Carol – "The school had a good atmosphere, you could sense it as you walked in the door, it was purposeful. There was a smart uniform. Everything was quite calm during lesson time, but of course, when the bell went, all hell was let loose. I taught there for seven years and I left in 1992. When it's going well, teaching is the best job in the world."

The school has had several changes of head-teacher over recent years. Mr Lowry was head-teacher until 1988 when he was followed by Mrs Morffew for three years. After Mrs Morffew left in 1991, she was succeeded by Mr Ellis until his retirement in 1996. Mrs Jill Rattle took over briefly until Mr Brian Pain was able to take up his post in 1997. When Mr Pain left in July 2000, Mrs Rattle again took charge until the present head-teacher Mr John Birchall came to the school in November 2000.

The Log Books of more recent years are unfortunately not as interesting as the older ones, giving details of endless visits from the 'nit nurse' and the school dentist, and problems with the boiler room flooding. Newspaper cuttings saved in a scrap book tell of various community activities which have involved pupils, such as parties for elderly people, knitting blankets for Romanian orphans in 1991, and the establishment of a 'Tidy Club' in 1990. This was a small group dedicated to taking a pride in the local area by picking up litter and its members were the driving force behind recycling and conservation projects. In 1992 three boys restored a neglected courtyard garden at the school and made a kitchen garden near the home economics room.

However, it is the unique school farm which has been able to give pupils a real insight into the natural environment. A hundred years ago most children lived in houses or cottages with gardens and domestic or farm animals nearby. The children of Millbrook, as the Log Books reveal, were country children. Many of them lived on farms and had to help their fathers after school, or they were sent to work in the fields. They knew all about growing things, and how food was produced, from their own experience.

'Down to Earth' farm buildings and the goats, 2000.

In the 1930s and '40s gardening was on the curriculum for all the boys and they made a substantial contribution to wartime school meals with produce from the farm.

By the 1950s and '60s things had changed a little. The boys who did gardening were allocated allotments and had to run them as a small commercial concern. They had to grow vegetables from seed sowing to harvest and sale. Pigs and poultry were kept and sent to market. Eggs and honey, as well as vegetables were sold, and the profits ploughed back into running expenses. There was a Southampton Secondary Schools Certificate, which was a very basic qualification for those who could not take academic examinations, and the boys who did the gardening and farm work took this test. At the time, agricultural work was considered a suitable occupation for those who were not very clever, but the course they took at Millbrook not only equipped them with practical skills and knowledge but gave them training in running a business as well.

Today the farm is a Local Education Authority resource and is known as the 'Down to Earth Centre'. Children from Infant and Junior schools all over Southampton, and further afield, visit the farm in connection with various National Curriculum studies. Until December 2001 the farm was managed by Bob Bull, who is one of the last teachers specifically trained and qualified in rural studies. There is a paid assistant, and a group of volunteers from the local community come in and help to care for the animals on a regular basis. Gardening is no longer a school lesson, although visits are made to the farm in connection with various aspects of the sciences. There is an 'after school' club for Millbrook pupils who are interested in caring for the livestock.

Today most children live in houses or flats with little or no garden, and caring for animals or growing plants is impossible. The 'Down to Earth' farm has a range of animals, chickens, sheep, pigs, a cow, ducks and goats. There are vegetable plots growing potatoes, cabbages, and tomatoes and specimen plantings of wheat and other cereal crops. Pupils from primary schools all over the city visit the farm to learn about spinning and weaving wool, grinding flour and baking bread. They see where eggs come from and discover that vegetables grow in soil. To children brought up entirely in towns this is new and exciting information.

The first Millbrook School was established in 1819, when King George III was on the throne. The school has taught generations of Millbrook children through the reigns of nine kings and queens; George III, George IV, William IV, Victoria, Edward VII, George V, Edward VIII, George VI and Elizabeth II. Life has changed a great deal in the 182 years since the school's foundation. At the beginning of the 21st century, the school continues to strive towards high standards and to equip the pupils for a constantly changing world.

BIBLIOGRAPHY

'Millbrook School Log Books' – Southampton City Archives.

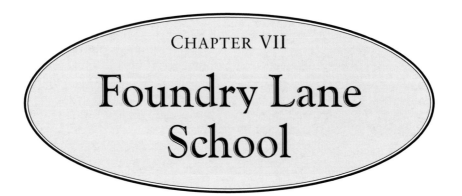

CHAPTER VII

Foundry Lane School

The foundation stone of Foundry Lane School was laid on 15 July 1901, and the school was opened the following year as Foundry Lane Board School. Unlike Millbrook and Redbridge schools, Foundry Lane was never a rural school. It was set up to educate the children who lived in the rapidly expanding suburbs of Southampton. They were children who lived in the small terrace houses which were being hastily built to provide homes for working men and their families. Their fathers worked in the docks or in the foundries and factories of the town, not on farms or in agricultural trades. It was an area where poverty was common.

Girls' Department

September 1st 1902

School opened today, number admitted 467.

November 10th 1902

During the absence of the teacher a girl stole a needlework bag belonging to the school and containing some knitting. She also came back into school after the teachers had gone and took some ribbon from cards hanging in the corridor. When the theft was discovered a policeman was sent for, who warned the girl and visited her parents. They expressed great concern and restored the knitting. The child at first denied all knowledge of the stolen articles, but on being caned, confessed to having taken them.

April 29th 1903

Subjects taught in school during the current year. Arithmetic, reading, composition, dictation, copy writing, singing by note, drill, history, geography, recitation, elementary science, object lessons, map drawing, needlework, scripture.

December 4th 1905

Free dinners have begun here today. A portable boiler for fifty basins of soup, basins and spoons, are being lent by Mr Etheridge. The soup is cooked by the caretaker, who sends over at 12 o'clock the amount required to each of the three departments.

Number of pupils on roll 694.

April 19th 1912

Expressions of sympathy with children affected by the Titanic disaster were read out according to instruction.

May 29th 1918

A nurse sent by Dr. Lander gave a lesson to the senior girls in washing and dressing a baby. The baby was kindly lent by one of the mothers.

Although the entries from the Log Books give an interesting insight into the activities of the school, the personal reminiscences of a past pupil, **Joyce Hillier**, bring the schooldays of the past vividly to life. Mrs Hillier returned to the school many years later and worked there as the secretary. When she retired in 1986 she studied the school records and produced a short history based on the Log Books.

"I was born in 1923, so I must have gone to Foundry Lane School in 1928 because we started school at five years old in those days. It wasn't terribly strict in the Infants', it could have been worse. We didn't get smacked or stood in the corner, but there was no playing with sand trays or water or anything like that, we had proper lessons. We had formal lessons in reading and writing and arithmetic.

"In the Infants the boys and girls were mixed, but when you got to about the age of seven you went up into the big Girls' School, which was a lot more strict. We wore navy blue gymslips and white blouses with a red and white tie. The girls were on the ground floor and the Boys' School was upstairs. You hoped you never had to meet the boys, those rough, uncouth boys. You used to dread the Headmistress sending you with a message, there were no telephones in those days. If they wanted some errand done the teachers would send someone who could 'hold their own' because you really had to run the gauntlet of those boys. We hated taking letters round to all the classes, they would whistle and shout at you.

"They were very particular about handwriting at Foundry Lane. We had this teacher called Miss Reed. She was very plump and she used to creep around the class and come up behind you and peer over your shoulder to see what you had done. She always carried an ebony ruler and if you'd got something wrong this ruler would suddenly whizz from behind you and whack down on your fingers. She was a real tartar, but I have to say that a lot of those girls were nice writers and still are. She surprised us utterly by getting married one day, we never dreamt she would do a thing like that.

"We used to write with pens with metal nibs, the sort you dipped into an inkwell on the desk. That was how I got myself into trouble one day. I was bored stiff listening to the teacher, it was a geography lesson I think, and I put an elastic band over the inkwell and sat there seeing how far I could stretch it. I didn't know the well was going to shoot up into the air and splash the ink all over the wall. I was thoroughly told off and sent to the caretaker's house for a bucket of hot water and a cloth and made to wash the wall down.

"We used to chant tables every day, it was the best way of learning them, I can still remember them today. Then we would have spelling tests and we had to learn poetry off by heart as well, I still have one of the books we had to learn from.

"We did have sewing lessons but not a great deal of it and of course we didn't have sewing machines at school so it was all hand done. We didn't make clothes or anything very useful, it was little bits of things to practise different stitches. We were taught how to sew a button on and how to do darning. I can still darn a sock properly with the loops round the edge of the hole. We learned plain sewing, useful sewing like making run-and-fell seams, French seams and hemming, not embroidery or fancy stitches. You have to remember that schools didn't provide all the materials and things that they do today. When we got older we had cooking lessons, but we had to go to the Western School for that because there weren't any facilities at Foundry Lane. We made fancy cakes, things like that, not meat dishes or proper meals.

"You left school at fourteen in those days unless you passed the Scholarship and went on to Grammar

Evacuation poster.

School. You just had the one opportunity of taking the exam, if you were ill on the day that was just too bad and you missed the chance of going to Grammar School. You didn't have to pay fees then, but it was still expensive for parents to buy uniform and the various things you needed. I left school when I was fourteen and took a commercial course."

September 27th 1938

Today members of the local Air Raid Precautions Service have taken possession of the two spare classrooms to assemble gas masks. These, when assembled, will be distributed to the homes of children with instructions for use.

August 31st 1939

We have received orders to evacuate on Saturday September 2nd at 6.30 a.m. We evacuate to Christchurch with about 170 children and all staff.

April 1st 1940

The Foundry Lane buildings are taken over by the Military Authorities. Our children move into huts at Regents Park School [*the ones who were not evacuated*]. Under the present arrangement the girls are on a double shift with the boys, mornings and afternoons alternate weeks. The girls attend at the huts for three hours daily, and at the Drill Hall, Stratton Road, twice a week for two hours, and at the recreation ground once a week for organised games.

September 9th 1945

This school re-opened this morning. Owing to the re-organisation of schools in Southampton, this school is now Foundry Lane Junior Girls' School. [*Previously it took pupils up to the school leaving age of fourteen.*]

September 26th 1952

Former pupils and staff held Jubilee celebrations this evening. Two trees were planted in the garden by Mr Gosham and Miss de Grouchy. Afterwards official guests and old scholars came into school for refreshments. The proceedings were brought to a close by the singing of the National Anthem. So fifty years of the school were commemorated.

July 1st 1962

Our portable swimming pool is in full use today.

January 14th 1963

Owing to the severe frosts and snow, which is still lying thickly on the ground after three weeks, the toilets are frozen. Classroom temperature is only 52 degrees.

The Girls' School closed in the summer of 1969 and Foundry Lane became a mixed school from the start of the new school year.

Boys' Department

September 8th 1902

School opened. It was built to accommodate 480 pupils, but 521 are registered.

September 19th 1902

A complaint has been made by a gentleman living nearby, that stones have been thrown at his cattle in the field. The whole school was warned against future offences of this kind.

May 29th 1903

At 3.45 p.m. on Thursday, boys with the admission fee of one halfpenny, a towel and bathing drawers, formed up and walked to the Corporation Swimming Baths. The drawers were made by the Girls' Department in their needlework classes and sold to the boys at cost price, one and a half pence per pair.

June 5th 1903

Forty boys who will take Cottage Gardening marched to Red Lodge Nursery and were shown around the gardens.

December 4th 1903

The frosty weather is making the distress among the poor very marked. I received a parcel of clothing from the mother of two ex-pupils and have fitted out two poorly clad pupils with the contents. A magic lantern entertainment was given on Friday evening on behalf of the Benevolent and Orphans Fund. Four Masters worked the lanterns and 120 boys each paid 1*d* admission. On making inquiries among 440 boys present on Monday, I have a list of 71 scholars whose parents are out of work.

January 2nd 1904

The distress is still prevalent, but by means of the Relief Committee many parents are helped and I found no boy who had come to school fasting, but two cases of absentees were reported as being without food. Arrangements have been made by which children with no food can be allowed to attend a Free Breakfast Centre at Shirley School. Sixteen boys are absent because they have no boots.

February 2nd 1904

A large number of old boots and shoes have been sent here from Handel College, [*a private school in the Polygon area*] and several cases of 'bad boots' have been relieved. Where none were found suitable, in deserving cases, five new pairs were fitted. I have sent letters to the higher-class schools regarding boots and have received second hand ones from St. Winifred's and the Grammar School [*King Edward VI School*], and Banister Park School. The bigger boys are also bringing left-off clothing for the smaller ones.

July 7th 1905

Cottage Gardening is taken at Red Lodge Nurseries [*The nurseries were in Winchester Road on the site of the modern Red Lodge School*], on Wednesday afternoons. In response to an application by me for prizes for Cottage Gardening, Messrs. Toogood and Son have written to say they will present a silver medal and two certificates.

June 30th 1911

Boys to the number of 510 attended the tea and Coronation festivities for King George V at Blighmont Park. The Mayor and Mayoress visited the grounds . A team of four boys from the school won the team race at the Coronation Sports on the Common and were each presented with a gold medal.

May 3rd 1912

Nine boys attending this school were affected by the Titanic disaster. George and Arthur Hawkesworth, Tom Nichols, Charles Johnson, Lois Hurst, Reginald and Christopher Biddlecombe, Jack Wormald and Tom Stebbings, all of whom lost a father.

August 21st 1914

Owing to war having broken out, Mr Hallam, a Master in this school, who is a sergeant in the 5th Hampshire Territorial Regiment, was absent on active service. The boys were addressed by me on their proper conduct during the war's progress and I suggested that those who knew of old Foundry Lane School boys who were engaged on active service should give their names to their class Master. A list of 70 names was compiled and posted up in school.

January 22nd 1915

During the morning there was no coal and the boys and staff ran around the playground to get warm before commencing work. On Thursday I asked each pupil at assembly to bring some little offering to help in the housekeeping at the hospital for wounded Belgian soldiers in Clifton Lodge, Regents Park Road. On Friday the collection was made. The potatoes weighed over 2 cwts. And the remainder consisted of turnips, swedes, carrots, beet, parsnips, onions, cabbages, bread, cakes, flour, rice, tea and sugar, while a few parents sent cigarettes and matches.

September 15th 1916

Mrs Hand [*assistant mistress*] received a telegram during lunchtime on Monday announcing the death of her brother, a soldier at the Front, and was so distressed that she was unfit for school duties that afternoon, but she was back at 9 a.m. on Tuesday.

January 19th 1917

On Tuesday I was not so well and thought a day in bed would help to get rid of my cold. During my absence two police officers called and arrested Mrs Mason, a member of staff, and took her away.

Mrs Mason, her husband, mother and aunt were all tried at the Old Bailey on a charge of conspiring to poison the Prime Minister, Mr David Lloyd George. They were active Socialists and very much opposed to conscription. Mrs Mason's mother, Mrs Alice Wheeldon, was a Suffragette. Mrs Mason's brother was a conscientious objector and whilst 'on the run' was arrested at her home in Millbrook Road. Mr and Mrs Mason were found guilty of conspiracy and sentenced to five years penal servitude, and Mrs Wheeldon to ten years.

January 16th 1918

On Thursday I received news of the death of Lieutenant Howard G. Hallam, a Master from this school. He was in recent heavy fighting around Jerusalem and while under fire was bending over one of his men bandaging him, when a bullet struck his shoulder, hit his spinal column and penetrated his lungs. He was in hospital at Port Said in a critical condition, being paralysed below the waist. He wrote cheerful letters, but at last succumbed to his injuries. I addressed the assembled school on his death, after a heroic deed truly characteristic of a British officer in action.

November 11th 1918

At 11.30 a.m. a letter was brought stating that on account of the Armistice being signed, the schools would be closed for the afternoon. The boys sang 'The flag of Britain' and gave three cheers for the King and dismissed.

May 24th 1923

Empire Day celebrations. The school assembled and listened to the 'Empire Day Record' consisting of the Coldstream Guards playing the National Anthem and 'Home sweet home'. The fine gramophone was lent by Captain Holt, brother of Mr. Holt of this staff. This was followed by their Majesties King George V and Queen Mary speaking to the children of the Empire.

March 31st 1924

I terminate my engagement on reaching retirement age today. I have been Head Teacher since the school opened in 1902. As parting gifts the staff and students presented me with a solid oak chair, a radiator, a kettle and a hall lamp.

Albert A. Fry.

April 1st 1924

Mr Tom Smith commenced duty as Head Teacher today.

April 28th 1924

Received notification from the Local Education Authority to discontinue gardening classes.

July 13th 1932

Beavis Treat, 121 senior boys visited Beaulieu, Christchurch and Bournemouth by motor coach.

The Beavis Treat was a high spot in every school year. After the First World War, Alderman William Beavis gave £10,000 to fund annual Treats for elementary school children, in memory of the sons of Southampton who had died in the war. Children were to be given a tea and a sports day on the Common. The first Treat was held on 23rd July 1920.

Fred Young, who attended Foundry Lane School 1925–1934 remembers the Treats.

"My memories of the Beavis Treat were that we went to Pirrie Park in Bellemoor Road, adjacent to where Taunton's College is now, and we indulged in 100 yard races, egg and spoon, and three-legged races. On one particular day when it was wet, we stayed in the classroom and played games, pitching a ball into a bucket and darts, and we had our tea and buns at our desks."

April 26th 1939

A crowded meeting of parents was held last evening when I addressed them on the objects, ways and means of the Evacuation scheme. Forms have been distributed to all children.

September 1st 1939

Evacuated to Christchurch

The teachers who accompanied the children when they were evacuated were asked to send a progress report to the Education Office in Southampton. These letters are in the City Archives. Mr R. Denness went to Bournemouth Senior School, whilst Mr Eric Barter supervised groups of Foundry Lane children at Wareham, Corfe Castle and Milborne St. Andrew. Girls were sent to Bransgore, Christchurch and Dorchester. In the first evacuation 115 boys and 140 infants and girls left Southampton.

Mr R. Denness – "The health of the children is excellent. With some exceptions the clothing question has solved itself with regards to the senior children owing to older boys taking out papers and so getting together funds to supply deficiencies both for themselves and younger brothers and sisters. The children have benefited from their stay in Bournemouth. Their manners are good out of school, they are clean and give little trouble to the neighbours. The Scouts, Cubs and St. John's Ambulance cadets have welcomed the children and encouraged them to join. Of the 150 children concerned in the first evacuation, at present no more than 20 of them are left. Reasons for withdrawal – homesickness, failure of billeting officer to provide satisfactory billets, parents recalling children due to no raids at home, cases of bedwetting."

Mr Eric Barter – "Local people, while quite willing to take children after a blitz, are not always agreeable to relieving their neighbours of them in times of comparative quiet.

"The most satisfactory billets are where the householder is of a similar social standing to that of the children's parents. The larger houses have not generally been so suitable, as while the children may be well looked after, they do not get accepted as members of the household owing to the differences in their habits and outlook. In the case of the smaller homes, the evacuees are often treated almost as members of the family. Cases of children never receiving visits from their parents have been very rare. One unsatisfactory aspect of the visits is that in some instances parents have arrived at weekends expecting to be fed and occasionally slept by the householders for very small payment, if any. Householders would welcome the parents if they would take into account rationing and other difficulties. A small minority of parents appear deliberately to withhold clothing in the knowledge, or hope, that the householders will provide it. A number of children were sent out badly equipped.

"Many of the evacuees have shown some improvement in character. I believe that a good deal is due to the greater facilities for boyish pursuits and recreation. Except for a case of apple stealing in the summer, none of the children has been in trouble with the police.

"At Christmas 1939, Beales of Bournemouth gave an excellent party and entertainment to all evacuees in the area, while cinema proprietors gave free shows and many local residents helped with gifts or amusements during Christmas week.

"Of 75 children evacuated to Corfe Castle in June 1940, only 11 remain. Of the 33 to Milborne St. Andrew only 12 are left. 50 per cent of those in Bournemouth have gone home. There appears to be a case for providing some means of deterring parents from withdrawing their children for trivial reasons. And treating the billeting scheme too casually."

February 19th 1940

Foundry Lane Boys' School opened at Regent's Park Infants, the boys attending part-time only. Air Raid Precautions – Classes A, B, and C are using Anderson shelters in people's gardens within three minutes of the school. Class D has use of the shelter in the playground. Practices of going to the shelters have been carried out until arrangements are quite satisfactory.

September 11th 1945

Foundry Lane Junior Boys' School opened today with 451 boys on roll.

January 29th 1947

Weather extremely bitter and heavy snow falling. Classroom temperatures as low as 29 degrees even with fires. Lavatory cisterns frozen. Attendance only 33 per cent.

February 8th 1952

The school listened to the proclamation of Queen Elizabeth II, His Majesty King George VI having died on February 6th.

July 27th 1952

Some 400 old scholars and staff attended to celebrate the 50th anniversary of the founding of the school.

November 16th 1953

A slow combustion stove fitted in each classroom, in place of the open fires.

November 3rd 1966

The sum of £5.10.0 sent to the Mayor for the Aberfan Disaster Fund.

September 11th 1968

School will commence with mixed classes

July 23rd 1969

Re-organisation of school completed in preparation for full amalgamation of Boys' and Girls' schools in September. Foundry Lane Boys' School came to an end after 67 years, to be replaced by Foundry Lane Junior Mixed School.

September 8th 1970

School opened in the new name of Foundry Lane Middle School with an age range of 8–12 years.

January 27th 1971

A meeting of parents was held to give them the opportunity of using the new decimal currency to come into use on February 15th.

January 8th 1974

In the country as a whole the three-day week is in operation as the result of the miners' overtime ban. In school restrictions apply on lighting and heating. Half-term holiday is to be extended to one week, caused by the fuel crisis owing to the miners' strike.

December 12th 1974

The re-union of pre-1914 pupils was held this afternoon. Approximately 104 pupils and 2 ex-teachers attended. Accounts were broadcast on the local television programmes and Radio Solent.

June 23rd 1977

An exhibition 1902–1977 was held to commemorate the Silver Jubilee of H.M. Queen Elizabeth II and the 75th anniversary of the school.

September 3rd 1979

Number on Roll 310

April 14th 1980

School meals cost 50p from today, numbers having them dropped by a half.

January 18th 1985

Extraordinarily cold weather freezes girls' toilet block, causing emergency closure of the school.

January 25th 1990

Storm damages Middle School roof, removing slates, gable and guttering. The huge tree in the south playground is swaying dangerously.

July 15th 1992

This is a special week to celebrate the 90th anniversary of the school. A playground party was held for all the children from First and Middle Schools, 400 children sat together at tables outside, sang songs and listened to the Bellemoor Boys' Band and ate mountains of food.

July 16th 1992

An evening re-union of pre-war pupils and staff was held. Pupils acted as guides. The oldest guest was 99 years young! As the present Head, I found the evening very uplifting and I feel proud to be the Head Teacher at Foundry Lane, a school with a great history which we continue today.

BIBLIOGRAPHY

Hillier, J. M.: *Extracts from Foundry Lane School.*
Wartime education documents in City Archives.

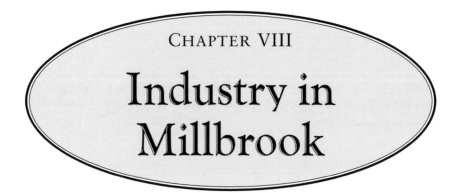

CHAPTER VIII

Industry in Millbrook

Mills, foundries and tanning

There has always been industry in Millbrook. From the earliest days it was centred on Tanners Brook, which supplied a reliable source of power. There were corn mills, tanneries, foundries and factories along its course and by the 19th century the Brook formed an industrial zone in the countryside.

The King's Charter of A.D. 1045 speaks of the grinden broc as one of the boundaries of Millbrook. Broc fairly obviously means brook, and grinden means grinding, thus we have a 'grinding stream' or mill brook. This stream must be Tanners Brook. So where was the mill in Millbrook? One possibility is that the mill referred to was Shirley mill, which stood at the cross roads of Romsey Road and Winchester Road and was powered by the confluence of Tanners Brook and Hollybrook. However, that mill is specifically mentioned in the Domesday Book of 1085 as being Shirley mill. This suggests that there was another mill.

The probable site of the Millbrook mill is at the junction of Oakley Road and Tebourba Way where a road-bridge crosses over the Tanners Brook. In Tebourba Way there is an entrance into a strip of woodland called Mill Mead Woodland Conservation Area. A few yards inside the gateway there is a culverted stream, which is now mainly stagnant, but was once the mill leat. The main Tanners Brook flows at a much lower level through the woodland. Originally a channel must have been dug somewhere near The Old Thatched House pub to divert water out of Tanners Brook and into the leat. Of course this has disappeared under the junction at Tebourba Way. The water flowed along the leat, through the water-mill, and then fell back down into the main Brook by the bridge in Oakley Road. It was known as Mousehole Mill. Nearby was Mousehole Farm and in fact Oakley Road used to be called Mousehole Lane until 1909.

The mill, which probably dated from medieval times, stood where Jayhard Plumbers Merchants stands today and would have been a corn mill. By 1843 the mill had been turned into a foundry which was in business until late Victorian times.

A few years later a paint factory was also established on the site by Captain George Peacock. He had developed an anti-fouling paint to prevent the hulls of ships becoming encrusted with barnacles. Captain Peacock was appointed Southampton dock master in 1848 and almost immediately went into partnership with H. J. Buchan to produce the anti-fouling compound and other varieties of marine paint. He made a great contribution to the British economy through the foreign sales of huge amounts of Peacock and Buchan's paints, made in Millbrook.[1]

Further down Tanners Brook, near the present Mill Road, there appears to have been another corn mill and by 1860, this too had become a foundry called the Vulcan Iron Works. The owner of the Works built a terrace of small cottages, Vulcan Terrace, for his workers. Vulcan Iron Works had become a varnish factory by 1897, and by the 1930s the factory was disused and the buildings were demolished to make way for Brookside Avenue.

Another corn mill was situated at the southern end of what is now called Foundry Lane, in the area between Somerset Terrace and Lakelands Drive. It was driven by a millstream which led from Freemantle Pond. Mill House stood roughly where Somerset Terrace is today. This mill also became a foundry, probably around 1809. It was bought by the Tickell brothers in 1818, and the cast iron 'Gas Column', which stands in Houndwell Park in Southampton, was manufactured at their factory. By 1824 the factory was in the ownership of Alexander Fletcher and John Young and was known as Mill Place Foundry.

In 1831 the foundry was bought by Ogle and Summers, who made steam carriages. Summers entered into partnership with Charles Day and John Groves a few years later when they started to build railway locomotives. Between 1837 and 1839 they produced at least three engines, Jefferson, Fly and Southampton. The firm also made marine engines and in 1836 the first iron steamship Forester was launched from Mill Place Quay. The wharf which served the foundry was opposite the end of Foundry Lane, immediately to the west of Millbrook station. Ships built at the foundry had to be dragged across Millbrook Road to be launched, and in 1839 road traffic was held up for several days whilst an iron steamship weighing 120 tons was moved. This difficulty led to the firm moving its shipbuilding activities to Northam in 1840 and the whole Millbrook foundry closed down in 1854, although the company, known as Day, Summers and Co. continued to prosper at the new site. The Millbrook wharf disappeared when land was reclaimed for the building of the New Docks in the 1930s.

Tanning (i.e. the processing of animal skins into leather), was another local industry, which gave its name to Tanners Brook. It was probably carried out as far back as the Iron Age when leather clothing was worn, but the first mention of anyone who worked as a tanner in Millbrook appears in October 1656. In a book of court cases brought before the mayor, Cornelius Williamson, a tanner, of Millbrook, complained that he had been robbed by a soldier, with whom he had spent the evening drinking.[2]

In 1809, in his *Companion in a tour round Southampton*, John Buller wrote that the process of tanning had long been carried out on Tanners Brook. The master Tanner from 1810 to 1843 was John Bridger, and he was succeeded by William Sharland. Workers from Sharland's tannery were housed in the buildings of the old Poor House after it had closed down. The trade went on late into the 19th century, a directory of 1887 lists Charles Gidden as a tanner and leather manufacturer, and Mr Butts and Mr Dawkins were both listed as boot makers.

A map of 1867 shows that there were brickfields and gravel pits in the vicinity of the Vulcan Iron Works and a sawmill is shown near Tanners Brook, between Millbrook Road and the railway line. Another sawmill stood on the corner of Green Lane and Romsey Road, it seems to have dated from the 1920s and was owned by Houghtons. **Marion Woolfe**, who attended the nearby Millbrook School in the 1940s, remembers collecting scraps of discarded timber to take home for firewood during the war. In July 1948 the sawmill caught fire and was burnt to the ground.

The Tobacco Factory

The British American Tobacco factory has been a feature of Millbrook life for 75 years and has been a major employer in the area. The development of the company makes interesting reading.

In 1901 the American Tobacco Company invaded the cigarette and tobacco market of Britain. The British manufacturers banded together and set up the Imperial

Tram at the Millbrook Station Terminus, 1940s. *From the collection of Bert Moody.*

Tobacco Company, and for a time both groups competed, but at great financial cost. In 1902 the two companies agreed to trade only in their home markets, and a new company, British American Tobacco, was set up to take over the export business of both firms.

The company extended its manufacturing activities to Southampton and in 1913 opened a factory in Blechynden Terrace. (After B.A.T. had left this site it was bombed during the Second World War. The ruins remain as a little memorial garden behind the Mayflower Theatre.) Larger premises were bought in 1916 at Albert Road near the docks and both factories worked until the Blechynden Terrace building was sold in 1921.

Then in 1925 B.A.T. bought 18 acres of land at Blighmont Park in Millbrook. Blighmont House and its immediate gardens were not included in the sale. At the time, Regents Park was still semi-rural with big country houses set in extensive grounds all along the road, but one by one they were being sold and speculative builders moved in. The Tobacco Company sold some of its land fronting on to Regents Park Road for housing, and by 1928 this was fully occupied.

The new factory was still under construction when, on 30 October 1926, the Albert Road premises caught fire and were destroyed. Although the Millbrook factory was not completed, the pace of work increased, and workers were actually able to move in and start production of cigarettes only six weeks after the blaze at Albert Road. It was a new and pleasant experience for the workers who transferred to the Millbrook factory. Instead of the crowded dockland area, they now worked in a quiet parkland setting, the Bramtoco Sports Club even started to make a cricket pitch in the grounds. Transport to work was conveniently provided by the No. 6 tram which ran to Millbrook station. (The service started in 1922 and closed down in 1947.)

These early days at the factory are remembered by **Grace Tweed** (nee Ward) who worked as a packer at the Millbrook site in the 1930s:

"I knew one or two other girls who worked at the tobacco factory, and I knew that they were paid fifteen shillings [75p] a week. That was a lot better than the five shillings [25p] you got working as a shop assistant, so I thought I would try to get a job there. I was fifteen.

"We had to start at eight o'clock in the morning and I had to get up to the top stairs to 'clock on'. We could have lunch in the canteen but I always liked to go home, it made a break. I had a good Mum, my meal was always ready on the table when I came in, and then I would cycle back for the afternoon shift. We worked from eight o'clock until six every day except Friday when we finished at five o'clock. On Saturday we came in from eight until twelve o'clock, and we had Sundays off.

"I always worked on the top floor in the packing room. We wore white overalls and there were five in a team at each table. There was one feeding the cigarettes into the machine, one making up the little packets, one packing the packets, and one boxing them off at the end of the table. The fifth one was kept busy sweeping up any waste and keeping it all tidy. You got used to the noise of the machinery but it was very tiring standing all day. All the dusty work with the loose tobacco was on the ground floor, we were only concerned with the cigarettes and packing them up into boxes. You had to feed the cigarettes into a hopper and then they came out on a belt and you picked them up by hand in fives and packed them into the packet, five, ten, fifteen, twenty. You had to keep up with the machine. Someone on the end of the table picked up the packets and put them into big cardboard cartons. The better the machine worked, the more money we earned because we got a bonus according to how much we produced. Of course, sometimes the machines broke down and then we didn't get so much.

"It was all girls or women doing the packing, but there were men doing heavy jobs like pushing the loaded trolleys and repairing the machines, the men's work. It was so noisy you couldn't really have a conversation, but we were all friendly. Most of the girls were quite nice and refined, but there were some who were a bit rough and ready and used to swear. I always hated cigarette smoking, I'd had enough of the smell of tobacco at work all day. Then the war came along and I left B.A.T. and went to become a trained nurse."

Fears of war grew, and in 1939 a new warehouse was hurriedly constructed so that stores of tobacco could be dispersed around the site, and all stocks would not be destroyed in one go if the factory was bombed. Before the warehouse floor was laid, a maze of brick tunnels was constructed to provide air raid shelters for the employees. It was thought they would be safe underneath a concrete floor and hundreds of cases of tobacco.

By August 1939, as war loomed closer, air raid precautions were planned. With practice, the workers could evacuate the factory and be in the shelter in four minutes. Covered ways were erected over paths to the shelter because it was thought that the packing room girls in their white overalls would make a conspicuous target from the air. The flat roof of the factory was usually covered in rain water, so bushes and branches were brought in and arranged on the roof to make it look like a lake from the air. The west wall of the factory was disguised with camouflage paint, reserve water tanks were installed, a military pill-box was built and a barrage balloon was anchored in the grounds.

It was all to no avail, the factory was hit in the first bombing raid on Southampton at 11 p.m. on 19 June 1940. The first bomb destroyed the White House Garage in Millbrook Road, and the second damaged the factory's lower Regents Park Road gate and shattered Mrs Marshall's sweet shop alongside.

During the Battle of Britain in the summer of 1940, air raid warnings were so frequent and prolonged, that on many days the staff spent more time sitting in the shelter than working. An ingenious plan was thought up to overcome this problem. Cunliffe-Owen's aircraft factory at Eastleigh had a direct line to the R.A.F. Fighter Command so that they could have early warning of approaching enemy raiders. So the B.A.T. Civil Defence officer established a 'hot-line' to Cunliffe-Owen's and using information provided by them, he could plot enemy movements on a big wall map. This meant he could delay sounding the alarm at the factory until the German bombers were actually within four minutes flying time of Millbrook. The public sirens were to be ignored, but once the internal alarms sounded, the staff had to move fast and get to the shelter.

In the Southampton Blitz of November 1940 both N and M warehouses were destroyed. Next day, listeners to the radio heard 'Lord Haw-Haw' announce that the smoke of burning tobacco high above Southampton could be seen from Cherbourg.

(Lord Haw-Haw, whose real name was William Joyce, was a traitorous Irish-American who broadcast propaganda messages from Germany. These were intended to alarm the British people and weaken morale. He often used very localised information like this to give the impression that the Germans had intimate knowledge about all British towns and particular targets.)

In 1941 another part of the factory was damaged, and then the warehouse which housed the shelter received a direct hit. Luckily this was a night-time raid and the only occupants were some local residents who were not badly injured. However, tobacco leaves were blown over a wide area and scattered all over nearby houses and gardens.

The destructive bombing of warehouses and factories across Britain had reduced the country's reserves of cigarettes to an alarming level. In those days the harmful effects of smoking had not been discovered and cigarettes were seen as being important to the morale of servicemen and civilians alike. The government decreed an urgent renewal of stocks and B.A.T. did its best to step up production.

Another way in which the factory helped the war effort was in the establishment of allotments in the grounds of the factory at Millbrook and 'digging for Victory'. Employees also set up a 'pig club'. A sty was built and pigs reared. From time to time they were slaughtered and pork was distributed amongst the members of the club who had looked after them.

In 1941 B.A.T. began to make an even more direct contribution to the war effort. Spitfire fighter planes were being fitted with reserve fuel tanks to extend their range over enemy territory. These tanks were always jettisoned over the sea before the plane returned to base, so there was a constant demand for new ones. The company negotiated a contract to make the tanks, no doubt in the hope of keeping their skilled machine engineers who might otherwise be transferred to more essential war work than making cigarettes. At a factory in Poole, the tanks were made by skilled workmen at a cost of £95 each. However, the B.A.T. engineer devised a production line method using the unskilled workers at Millbrook. Over three hundred girls were employed on fuel tank manufacture and one hundred and thirty top quality tanks were produced each week costing £5 per tank. Morale was kept high with 'Music while you Work' broadcast throughout the factory every day and E.N.S.A. (Entertainment National Service Association) concerts at lunch times. Wartime stars Ben Lyon and Bebe Daniels appeared on one occasion.

In the months leading up to D-Day, in 1944, an anti-aircraft gun was set up on the roof of one of the warehouses. The Commanding Officer of the unit in charge of the gun claimed that a giant Californian Redwood tree in the grounds, dating from the Blighmont House days, would obscure his view. Two black American soldiers billeted nearby climbed up the tree on his instructions and lopped off the top, much to the fury of the director of B.A.T.

After the war, once initial difficulties over the replacement of machinery and a shortage of packaging materials had been overcome, the factory was gradually modernised. New technology and automation were introduced, staff rooms, an attractive canteen and an up to date kitchen were housed in new buildings. Blighmont House, now dilapidated and overgrown, was bought by the company in 1962. The house was in a poor state and useless to the company, so it was unceremoniously demolished and the gardens disappeared under buildings. In 1967 Toogood's Seeds company closed down and its premises were offered for sale. B.A.T. bought the old seed trial grounds lying between their own factory and Millbrook Road and thus extended their site to 23 acres.

In 1970, 'C' warehouse, which had been hastily erected just before the war, was demolished and the area made into a car park. The old air raid shelters were left beneath the surface. The Toogood's seed trial grounds were briefly brought back into vegetable production to supply the canteen in 1976. Unfortunately this was the year of the exceptionally hot summer and prolonged drought, so the scheme was rather a failure and the land was soon covered in tarmac and turned into a car park. To commemorate the company's 75th anniversary in 1977, B.A.T. gave a gift of trees to Southampton and red oaks were planted along Tebourba Way.

Innovations such as bio-filters to minimise emissions, noise control measures, and a £230 million investment in manufacturing technology, have made the Millbrook factory one of the most advanced in the world. The Southampton site is B.A.T.'s third largest factory and all production is for export. Over 1,000 people are directly employed at the factory, plus many subcontractors. In the year 2000, B.A.T. claimed to generate £70 million for the local economy.

However, the year 2001 was to bring bad news for the factory. A European Parliament ruling was made banning the production and export of high-tar cigarettes in the European Union. The Millbrook factory's output was almost entirely of this type of high-tar cigarette for mainly Far Eastern markets. There was vigorous opposition because of the loss of 2,000 jobs at the factory and another 6,000 jobs in packaging and distribution across the region. The *Daily Echo* reported on 15 May 2001:

"Bosses at the giant British American Tobacco factory in Southampton have finally accepted defeat from the Euro M.P.s who condemned thousands of southern jobs to the scrapheap ... as the legislation gets its third and final reading in the European Parliament. B.A.T. officials now say it is highly likely that at least part of their production will move to the Far East."

Toogood's Seed Merchants

British American Tobacco took over the grounds of Toogood's Seed Merchants in 1967, and this firm too was an old-established Millbrook business. The firm was established in 1815, although whether it originated at the Millbrook site is not clear. Toogood and Sons Ltd. were holders of royal appointment as seedsmen to successive sovereigns since 1884. The Toogood family lived at Blighmont Lodge.

The distinctive brick building, which dates from 1920, still stands in Millbrook Road, although it is now occupied by the Solent Business Centre. Over the main doorway an inscription reads, 'Toogood and Sons, by appointment, the King's Seedsmen'. The business was run by the family over several generations, Tom and Ted Toogood being in charge in the 1940s. The firm was noted for the quality of its seeds and supplied farms and market gardens both locally and nationally. Behind the packing factory and office block there was a large area of land used as a trial ground for developing better hybrids and also as a seed-growing nursery.

Margaret Milsom worked in Toogood's trial grounds from 1944 to 1950. Although initially untrained and inexperienced, she was instructed by the Head Gardener, Mr. William Land, in the best techniques of gardening and propagating.

"I started out in the trial grounds, hoeing and digging and weeding. We were experimenting with Sweet Peas, trying to hybridise them and breed bigger flowers, sweeter perfume, and different colours. After a few months I was moved into greenhouse work where we grew tomatoes and cucumbers for their seed. We had to pollinate all the cucumber flowers by hand and make sure the atmosphere was kept at the right temperature and humidity. The tomatoes were allowed to ripen and then they were picked and dried before we could take the seeds out. We also had outdoor cold frames for growing melons for seed. The large brick building was a packing factory and all the seed was sorted and packeted in there. Although we grew a lot of vegetable seeds on the premises we had to buy in stocks of seeds from other producers as well to meet demand.

"Toogoods had a shop in Southampton town centre where they sold plants for the house, and bedding for the garden, as well as seeds. We grew a lot of pot plants for the Christmas market, I had a whole greenhouse full of gloxinias, and we took orders for chrysanthemums. We would start the chrysanthemums off outside and then transfer them into the greenhouse to bring them on for Christmas. I learned all about dis-budding and taking cuttings and the techniques of propagating chrysanthemums. We used to exhibit them in flower shows at the Avenue Hall in Southampton, and that was interesting because I met all sorts of people from the gardening world.

"Whilst I worked at Toogood's I used to go over to Millbrook station and tend the flower- beds along the platforms, that was part of my job."

REFERENCES

1. Panell, J. P. M.: *Old Southampton Shores.*
2. Thomson, S.: *Book of Examinations and Depositions Before the Mayor 1648–1663.*

BIBLIOGRAPHY

Leonard, A. G. K.: *More Stories of Southampton Streets.*
Batchelor-Smith, L.: *Loom of Memories.*

An advertisement for Toogood's seeds. *Southampton City Archives.*

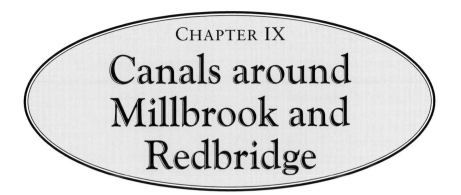

CHAPTER IX
Canals around Millbrook and Redbridge

by Peter Wilkinson

The 18th century saw the Industrial Revolution gathering momentum and manufacturers and traders began to look for ways of transporting their goods more easily than by the age-old method of horse and cart. Roads were still rough and difficult to use in winter, despite the construction of the Turnpike routes. Engineers and entrepreneurs began to consider the use of waterways for transport and set about making networks of canals connecting up rivers across the country.

Ambitious plans were made for connecting Redbridge and Andover. A canal was fully opened in 1795, the water being provided by the rivers Test and Anton. This canal was twenty-two miles long and had twenty-four locks, with a fall to sea level of 179 feet. It was large enough to take barges of 65 feet by eight and a half feet. The entrance to the canal at Redbridge was just a little up-river from the old Red Bridge, where a tide-lock was situated. This lock was demolished when the railway was built during the early 1860s. The canal ran parallel to the River Test, northwards towards Nursling, Lee and Romsey, passing close to Timsbury, through Horsebridge and Stockbridge, before reaching the south side of the River Anton at Andover.

Slates, coal and manure were carried up from Redbridge, whereas a variety of agricultural produce was transported down. However, trade was not good enough for the owners to pay off their loan interest and they were still in debt in 1851. The company became the Andover Canal Railway Company in 1857, and the canal navigation was closed in the autumn of 1859. At many points the canal bed was used by the railway, which was opened to Romsey in 1865.

In 1796 work was begun on a canal that was to run from Salisbury (Milford) to Southampton. This canal was to use nine miles or so of the existing Redbridge to Andover canal, with two arms, one from Kimbridge to Salisbury, the second from Redbridge to Southampton. From the junction at Kimbridge the canal was to pass through Lockerley, across Alderbury Common and then run parallel to the River Avon to Milford. This section was never quite completed and by 1803 was only navigable as far as the thirteenth lock on Alderbury Common. There was no longer any traffic on either arm of the canal beyond 1807. A lack of money and of traffic caused its end.

The section to Southampton left the Andover Canal at Redbridge, just a few hundred yards north of the tide-lock of the latter. It then passed around the eastern side of Redbridge village, before turning south to run along the shoreline towards Millbrook Point. From Millbrook the canal ran towards Four Posts Hill, still hugging the shore until it reached the Marlands, where the Civic Centre now stands. A tunnel was dug to take the canal under the parks towards Houndwell. On emerging from the tunnel at Houndwell the canal ran south towards the docks with a branch going northeast to Northam Quay.

The southern section passed along the eastern ditches of the medieval town, then beneath God's House Tower before emerging near Town Quay into the River Test. The Redbridge to Southampton section was only navigable as far as the western end of the Marlands tunnel and there is no record of the tunnel or the stretches to Northam and Town Quay ever being used.

Traces of this canal can still be seen running between the end of the up platform at Redbridge station and Old Redbridge Road, where the bed is still filled with water. It becomes visible again on the northern side of Redbridge roundabout where it forms a dip in the grassy area in front of bungalows along the western side of Gover Road. This dip is often waterlogged. Gover Road itself was built on one bank of the canal, the bungalows on the other.

There was adverse criticism at the time of the building of the Redbridge to Southampton section of the canal, the critics finding it absurd to build a canal next to the shoreline, when the River Test was itself navigable up as far as Testwood Mill. The critics no doubt felt vindicated by the short eleven-year life of this project. The then Poet Laureate, Henry Pye, who lived near Southampton, published the following verse:

Southampton's wise sons found their river so large,
Tho' t'would carry a ship, t'would not carry a barge.
But soon this defect their sage noddles supply'd,
For they cut a snug ditch to run close by its side.
Like the man who, contriving a hole through his wall,

To admit his two cats, the one great, t'other small,
Where a great hole was made for great puss to pass through,
Had a little hole cut for his little puss, too.

The railways would soon overtake the canals as the best means of transport, and canal projects were doomed.

BIBLIOGRAPHY

Rance, Adrian: *Southampton, an illustrated history.*
Vine, P. A. L.: *Hampshire Waterways.*

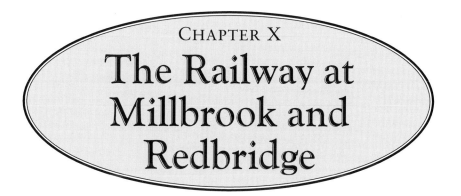

CHAPTER X
The Railway at Millbrook and Redbridge

by Peter Wilkinson

Before the Victorian Age the fastest means of transport was on horseback. The wealthy might ride in a carriage behind a team of horses, but for the majority of people, travel progressed at no more than the speed they could walk or a carter's horse could amble along. This meant that people seldom went far from their own village, a journey was a major undertaking not to be embarked upon lightly. The coming of the railway changed all this. The train could travel at incredible speed along its own iron road, covering great distances and carrying heavy loads, beyond the limits of any horse. Towns and isolated villages could be connected, farm produce could be taken to cities, and manufactured goods transported around the country.

The railway came to Southampton on 11 May 1840 when the line from London Nine Elms to Southampton was opened by the London & South Western Railway.

In June 1847 the railway between the towns of Southampton and Dorchester began to operate from Blechynden station, which was later called Southampton West and was eventually renamed Southampton Central in 1935. The railway line ran alongside the water's edge from Blechynden to Redbridge before crossing the River Test and going on to Eling Junction (Totton station). Initially this part of the line was double track, but the remainder to Dorchester was only single. The winding route to Dorchester via Brockenhurst, Ringwood and Wareham was nicknamed 'Castleman's Corkscrew' after the Wimborne solicitor Charles Castleman who promoted the line. No station was provided in Millbrook at this stage, but Redbridge station was opened with the line.

Millbrook railway station in the early 1920s. *Photograph by Lens of Sutton.*

On 1 November 1861, thanks to pressure from local residents, a small station was opened at Millbrook opposite the end of Foundry Lane, where Millbrook Road came closest to the line. At first, passengers at Millbrook were served by five trains each way on weekdays, then by 1869 six trains each way and three each way on Sundays. In 1894 the cost of a third-class ticket from Millbrook to Southampton West was 1*d*!

The goods yard was developed after 1907 from a siding connected to the western end of the station. Gradually the yard was enlarged and by 1928 there were nine sidings, a new goods office and a large warehouse. Holden & Sons had a coal order office in the yard, and Lisle's and Sibley's were two other coal merchants who operated there. Toogood & Sons, the seed merchants, whose premises were in Millbrook Road close to the station, also provided the yard with a considerable volume of traffic.

Just outside the station was the terminus of a tram-line which ran east along Paynes Road and Waterloo Road. The route continued via Four Posts Hill and Junction towards the docks, the No. 6 terminating by the South Western Hotel and the 6A at the Royal Pier. This branch was opened on 5 January 1922, closed to passengers in October 1935, but continued with workmen's services until 1947. Enthusiasm for trams remains undiminished for those who formed the Tram 57 Project, which has been based in Millbrook since 1979. They have been busy restoring two Corporation tramcars, the first to be re-discovered being No. 57. Both trams belong to Southampton City Heritage.

Millbrook station was remodelled in 1935 when other improvements included the quadrupling of the track and the laying of two extra lines to give access to and from the New Docks. The new station building was sited on an island platform with access across a new bridge.

In 1966 the station became unstaffed and the buildings were removed in 1968 because of vandalism. A small waiting shelter was subsequently provided. The goods yard which handled coal, cement and scrap metal was closed on 15 July 1967, the traders having to move elsewhere. Millbrook goods yard was re-developed as a Freight-liner Terminal which opened on 29 January 1968 and is still in use today, handling domestic and some container traffic.

Redbridge station opened with the line on 1 June 1847, in expectation of plenty of rail traffic. The present station building on the up platform is original. Redbridge station came under the control of the Millbrook station master in 1927. The track just west of the station divides, the Dorchester line curving left to cross the River Test, whereas the line which forks to the right goes to Romsey. This was opened on 6 March 1865 along with the extension to Andover, whose junction was at Kimbridge.

The railway brought increased industrial activity to the area. Timber handling and ship building were traditional activities at Redbridge long before the railway arrived. South Western oil-cake mill was one of the first factories in 1849, followed by Dixon and Cardus animal feeds. In 1863 there was a Vitriol works making artificial manure and lime, and in 1897 the Schultz gunpowder factory was built near the disused canal. This factory was taken over by the Royal Navy in 1914 and closed down in 1922. In 1880 the London and South Western Railway Company bought Redbridge Wharf and adjoining land, including the timber yards, sawpits, sheds, offices, stores and the mudflats and built the Permanent Way Works . Fir, pine or redwood sleepers imported from the Baltic and Canada were unloaded from cargo boats and barges at Redbridge Wharf.

The timbers were seasoned and then treated with creosote by hand and later under pressure in large autoclaves. Railway track needs a range of iron castings and in 1924 a foundry was set up at the Works, this later expanded into the disused Schultz site in 1933.

During World War II the railway equipment pro-duced in the Works was vital to the country and many women were drafted in to take over heavy manual jobs previously undertaken by men. The Permanent Way Works itself became a target for enemy action and on 19 June 1940 a high explosive bomb destroyed 7,000

Women working at the Permanent Way Works during World War II. *Photograph courtesy of Associated British Ports, Port of Southampton.*

stored railway sleepers and damaged the wharf and buildings. In 1943 additional tracks were laid from Redbridge to the New Docks in order to handle the increased war-time traffic, thereby allowing trains to run directly to and from the Bournemouth and Salisbury lines. These connections were removed ten years later.

The Permanent Way Works was continually keeping up-to-date with new developments and went over to the production of concrete sleepers and the manufacture of long welded rail, with new cranes and loading facilities being built in 1982. However, the foundry was closed down in 1988, closely followed by the rest of the Works in 1989.

BIBLIOGRAPHY

Fairman, J: *Making Tracks*.

Moody, Bert: *Southampton Railways*.

Petch, Martin: *Southampton Tramways*.

Mitchell, Vic and Smith, Keith: *Andover to Southampton*. 'Country Railway Routes'.

Dendy Marshall, C. F., revised by R.W. Kidner: *History of the Southern Railway*.

CHAPTER XI
The New Docks and Container Berths

by Peter Wilkinson

At one time Millbrook was a waterside village. Fishermen pulled up their boats on the shingle beach, and in more recent years pleasure boats sailed from the hard. Then in 1923, just a few months after Southern Railway had assumed ownership of the docks, Parliament sanctioned plans for a new area of docks to be built on four hundred and seven acres of reclaimed land. This was the beginning of drastic and irrevocable change in Millbrook.

There have been two major developments in Southampton Docks which directly affected Millbrook and Redbridge: Firstly, the Extension Quay or New Docks which stretched from the Royal Pier to Millbrook Point, and secondly, the Container Port which was constructed on a site between the King George V Graving Dock and Redbridge Causeway, beginning in 1967.

The present-day Mayflower Park became the construction site for the New Docks. Work began in January 1927 and continued in stages over a period of years. By autumn 1932 the first section of quays and transit sheds was complete and the four-funnelled *Mauretania* was the first ship to berth alongside on 19 October of that year. Rank's Solent Flour Mill was the first factory to occupy the site in 1934.

The King George V Graving Dock (the verb 'to grave' means to clean a ship's bottom by burning off accretions and tarring), was built at the Millbrook end of the new docks estate. It was officially opened by HM King George V on 26 July 1933, the king and queen arriving in the graving dock on the royal yacht *Victoria and Albert*. It was the largest dry dock in the world, being 1,200 feet long and 135 feet wide at the entrance, with a holding capacity of fifty-eight million gallons of water. Fittingly, the first ship to use the dry dock was the *Majestic* of the Cunard White Star Line in January 1934, at that time the largest liner in the world. A second dry dock was planned alongside, but was never built.

The liners *Queen Elizabeth* and *Queen Mary* have always held a special place in the hearts of Southampton seafarers and dockers. Retired dock worker **Ron Williams** describes how the two Queens were overhauled in the Millbrook Graving Dock.

"The Graving Dock up at Millbrook was the only dry-dock big enough to take the Lizzie and the Mary. They were laid up twice a year, they had a summer re-fit around August and the winter re-fit was in November. You had one following the other in, so that they always had one in service. The Graving Dock was built specially for those big liners. The *Queen Mary* was 81,000 tons and the Lizzie was 83,000 tons. The winter re-fit was to strip all the stuff out, all the furnishings came off. That all went over to Woolston, the building is still there behind Thornycrofts, but it's closed now. The upholsterers and seamstresses would overhaul the carpets and furniture, they didn't throw it away and have new all the time. The Yanks were the chewing gum boys and the gum used to get into the carpets and spoil them, so the repair girls would cut out a little hole and sew in a plug of carpet the same colour. The carpets weighed tons, we had to use the cranes on the stern to lift them ashore to be taken away for cleaning. The girls would take it apart into sections and there used to be dozens of men to roll it up and carry it out.

"I used to go with the riggers, or the chain gang as we called them, they're the dock bottom men. We would get the propellers off, a guy called Jack Holloway was in charge of that. We weren't allowed to speak or make a noise when that was being done because Jack had a whistle to signal to the winch drivers, 'Heave,' or 'Slack'. They'd be dropped down to the bottom of the dock and then the fifty-ton crane would haul them up onto the quayside to be overhauled. Then we'd draw the propeller shafts out. They were all fitted in a very hard wood called lignum vitae, and they would be re-packed and greased and cleaned and slotted back in.

"The bottom of the ship was cleaned and painted. They used to take about 50 tons of barnacles off the bottom of those ships. In those days there would be

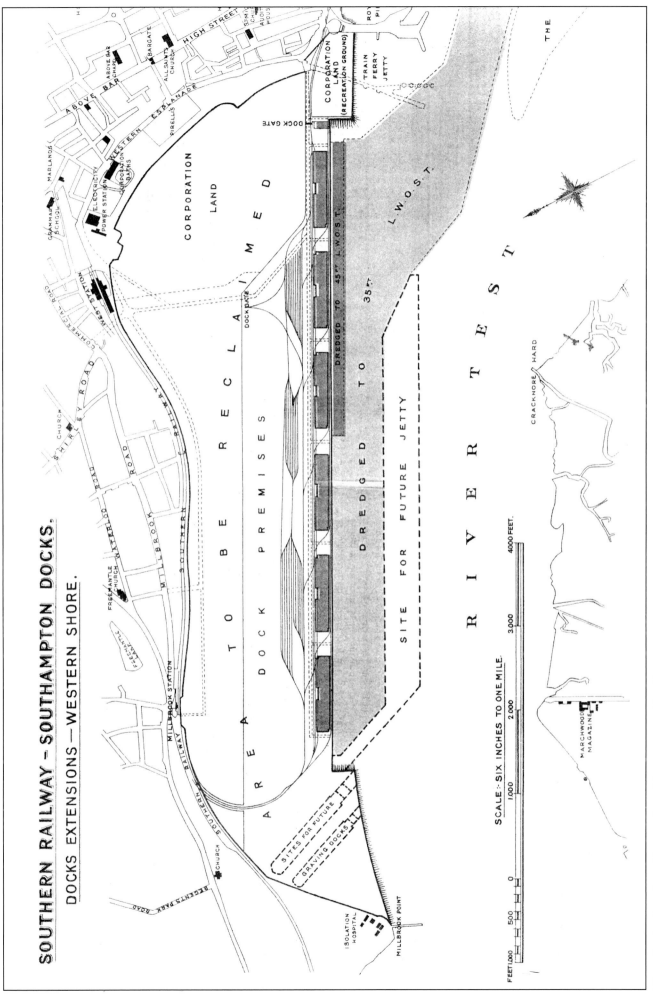

SOUTHERN RAILWAY—SOUTHAMPTON DOCKS.

DOCKS EXTENSIONS—WESTERN SHORE.

Plans for land reclamation work and the proposed berths. *Associated British Ports, Port of Southampton.*

SCALE:- SIX INCHES TO ONE MILE.

61

dozens of little flat-bottomed boats all tied together around the hull of the ship as soon as she came into the Graving Dock. All the cleaners and rough painters would be in these boats, there would be three or four hundred men. Then, as they pumped the water out of the Dock, the boats would gradually go down and they'd scrape and clean the bottom with wire brushes as they went. Today they do it with high- pressure hoses and they don't need all the workers. The Dock could be emptied quite quickly but they used to regulate the pumping to allow time for the scraping. When it came to painting, the same men would start at the top of the funnels being lowered down on planks, then they'd go over the side and gradually paint all the way down.

"It was a fascinating thing to watch the complete re-fit. There were two firms involved, Harland and Wolff and Thornycrofts. Everything was timed perfectly. If they said she was going to sail out of dry dock at 10 o'clock Monday morning, you could go on board say at 7.30 a.m. and the night gangs would be coming off and there would be pipes and hoses and tools all over the place. But you could stand there with your watch, and come 10 o'clock everything was painted and clean and tidy and she was ready to go. They were sticklers for time. There was no pressure, everyone had their job and they did it. There were hundreds, no, thousands, of men employed. Not like today, now everything is made in factories and just brought aboard, in the past you had the craftsmen. When the *Queen Mary* was being re-fitted after the war, she'd been used as a troop ship, you had craftsmen putting everything back just as it had been, there were men doing gold leaf and

artists working, it was fascinating to watch it going on."

The berths numbered 101 to 109 and four of the transit sheds were completed in 1934, but it was a few years before all the land was reclaimed and developed as an industrial site. The main railway and road access was finished by 1938.

In the late 1930s the New Docks at Millbrook were involved in an exciting, glamorous and relatively new means of transport. Flying boats were first used for passenger flights from Southampton just after the end of the First World War, when Supermarine Aviation converted Admiralty A.D. flying boats into 'Channel Type' four-seaters. On 16 August 1919 the Mayor of Southampton, Alderman S. G. Kimber (later Sir Sidney Kimber) and other dignitaries were invited by Mr Hubert Scott-Paine, Chairman of the Supermarine Aviation Company, to inaugurate a flying boat service from a terminal adjacent to the Royal Pier. The flight, piloted by Commander B. D. Hobbs, D.S.O., D.F.C., took them over the Isle of Wight. Supermarine provided flights to Cowes, Ryde, Totland Bay, Bournemouth and Southsea. Soon afterwards Le Havre was included in the list of destinations. Between 1923 and 1929 British Marine Air Navigation, a joint venture by Supermarine and the Southern Railway, began regular flights to Guernsey. In April 1924 this company was merged into Imperial Airways.

Then in 1937 the flying boat terminal was established in the New Docks, as Southampton became the operational centre for the 'Empire Air Mail Scheme'. On 29 June 1937 the Empire Service began with a flight to Durban, South Africa. This service was

The Queen Elizabeth in the King George V Graving Dock during her refit after wartime service in August/September 1946. *Photograph courtesy of Ron Hancock, Associated British Ports, Port of Southampton.*

operated from a pontoon off 101 berth by Imperial Airways with a fleet of 28 'C' class flying boats (monoplanes). The network of routes was quickly expanded to include Calcutta, Singapore, Cairo, Bahrain and Mombasa, as well as flights across the Atlantic. In 1938 a new wooden terminal, Imperial House, with passenger lounges and offices was built at 108 berth near the Graving Dock in Millbrook.

The outbreak of war in September 1939 saw the end of flying boat operations in the New Docks, and although BOAC re-opened the service in 1948 with a new terminal at 50 berth in the Eastern Docks, their operations ceased only two years later on 3 November 1950.

Subsequently Aquila Airways took over the air terminal left empty by BOAC, providing flying boat services to Genoa, Las Palmas, Lisbon and Madeira. Sadly, in September 1958, a lack of replacement aircraft brought the venture to an end.

During the Second World War bombing raids, especially from 30 November to 2 December 1940, caused extensive damage in the city and the docks. Amongst others, the Royal Pier was hit, while the new transit shed at 102 berth was destroyed and Solent Mills damaged.

The New Docks played their part in the preparations for D-Day, the King George V Graving Dock and adjacent quays being used for constructing bombardons. In 1944 there were serried ranks of landing craft,

The B.O.A.C. building at 108 berth. *Photograph courtesy of Associated British Ports, Port of Southampton.*

launches, U.S. Army Transport Corps railway wagons and armed fishing vessels alongside berths 101 to 110.

Parts of the Mulberry Harbours were built in the Graving Dock and at the western end of the docks. Thirty-nine sets of pontoons were constructed near the dry dock, and to the west of it, a train ferry terminal was sited for shipping engines and rolling stock across to France. The New Docks became one of the main embarkation points for the invasion of occupied Europe, with over four million troops passing through the whole port of Southampton.

In 1952 the Union Castle Line decided to build a new

Vessels moored at 108 berth in the New Docks prior to D-Day. The entrance to the King George V Graving Dock can just be seen on the left of the picture. *Hallett Jerrard Collection, Southampton City Cultural Services.*

two-storey terminal on the site of the war-damaged shed at 102 berth. This was officially opened in January 1956 and served the Union Castle Mail ships to South Africa. The first ship to use the new facilities was the *Edinburgh Castle*. The ships of the Union Castle Line sailed regularly at 4 p.m. on Thursdays, arrivals being on Fridays. When the *Southampton Castle* sailed on 16 September 1977, this marked the end of the Union Castle mail service, a service which had started one hundred and twenty years earlier under the Union Steamship Company.

A familiar sight for the residents of Millbrook was the *Queen Mary* in the King George V Graving Dock undergoing her annual summer overhaul. The *Queen Mary* sailed for the last time from Southampton on 31 October 1967 for Long Beach, California, and is now used as a tourist attraction. How sad it is that this beautiful liner wasn't kept in Southampton as a memorial after her many exploits in both peace and wartime, 31 years of service!

The *Queen Elizabeth* should have begun service from Southampton in 1940, but because of the war she arrived in Southampton for the first time on 20 August 1945, sailing on her maiden commercial voyage on 16 October 1946. She sailed for the last time in November 1968 and was sadly destroyed by fire in Hong Kong harbour in January 1972. Her successor, the *Q.E.2*, made her maiden voyage to New York on 2 May 1969.

By the early 1960s passenger traffic had declined to the extent that it became clear to the British Transport Docks Board, who had assumed control from the British Transport Commission, that the future of the port lay in cargo operations. They decided to construct a new container port, choosing a site between the King George V Graving Dock and Redbridge Causeway.

This project required the reclamation of mudflats at a cost of sixty million pounds. The first stage was authorised in January 1967 and dredging work began the following month. Belgian Line's *Teniers* was the first ship to use the new berth, number 201, in October 1968, which was adjacent to the Graving Dock. A second berth was completed in January 1972, followed by the Maritime Freightliner Terminal in March, constructed within the container port. By this time the second stage of the project had begun, which entailed building more berths towards Redbridge, covering eighty and a half acres of reclaimed land. Two of these berths became operational in 1973, the last, No. 206, being finished early in 1978. Royal consent was obtained in 1979 to name the area the Prince Charles Container Port. Meanwhile, in January 1968 Millbrook goods yard had been remodelled as the first Freightliner Terminal, where containers are transferred from road to rail.

Berths 201 and 202 are no longer container ship berths, but have become roll-on/roll-off car terminals. Since 1978 the container port, run by Southampton Container Terminals (S.C.T.) has expanded by one additional berth, No. 207, which was completed in December 1996 at a depth of 15 metres. The number of units handled per annum has increased dramatically since 1973 from approximately 160,000 'teus' to 1,068,000 in the year 2000. The capacity of a container ship is measured in 'teus' or 20 equivalent units, that is to say, the number of 20-foot containers or equivalent that the ship can hold.

There is no more space for the container port to expand, but the area for storing containers is being re-designed and ever-bigger cranes and straddle carriers bought. Container ships are growing in size which means that the berths must be dredged to greater

The Maritime Freightliner Terminal in 2001. Holy Trinity Church is in the background. *Photograph Peter Wilkinson.*

depths. At the time of writing S.C.T. have cranes that can reach 17 and 18 containers wide to load and unload ships on the quayside. New cranes that can reach 20 containers wide are on order.

The majority of containers are 20 or 40 feet in length, eight feet wide and eight feet six inches high. There are various types of containers, among them refrigerated ones with their own motors for transporting food-stuffs, containers with air vents for dry foodstuffs and tank containers for carrying bulk liquids. Seventy-five per cent of the containers imported contain high-tech and low-tech goods from the Far East. Amongst the goods exported are chemicals, tyres, steel and foodstuffs.

Sixty-three per cent of containers are transported to or from the terminal by lorry. Each day about one thousand container lorries arrive at the terminal. Thirty-two percent of containers are transported by train from two rail Freightliner terminals. Ten trains arrive and depart each day from the Freightliner ter-minal in the port and three each day from the terminal at Millbrook station. The remaining five per cent of containers travel by 'feeder ships' which bring con-tainers from other European ports to meet the 'mother' vessels in Southampton.

The straddle carriers are the tall crane-like vehicles that carry containers from one place to another inside the container terminal, for example to and from the storage areas to the lorries and trailers as well as to the quayside. The majority of straddle carriers are thirteen metres high, although the new ones are 16 metres high. They can lift one container over two or three more stacked on top of one another and have a lifting capa-city of forty tonnes. They straddle the container and lift it by means of a frame called a 'spreader' which has special hooks and twist-locks. These lock onto the reinforced corners of the container.

This modern system of computerised cargo handling can load and discharge 20,000 tonnes of containers in less than 24 hours, whereas the pre-container system needed twenty days to handle the same tonnage of general cargo.

Ron Williams, a retired foreman docker, describes the stevedores' conditions of employment:

"Before the war, stevedores had to go down to the docks early in the morning and the foreman would choose a number of men for a day's job, usually his pals, and give them each a metal 'tally' which they had to present at the wages office to get their money. If he needed more men to make up the team he would throw a handful of 'tallies' in the air and they would all scramble and try to grab one so that they could have a day's work. There used to be fights, men got desperate. Men could be employed for as little as an hour unloading baggage from a passenger liner, then they'd be paid off and had to go back to the docks office to try to get another job.

"After the war, in 1948, they had a new system,

A massive crane in the Container Port, 2001 *Photograph Peter Wilkinson.*

and the National Dock Labour Board was set up. The N.D.L.B. employed you and the shipping lines hired labour from the Board. At first you still didn't get paid if there was no work, but then they brought in the 'bumping' system. They used to 'bump' your card, stamp it. All the shipping lines paid money into a kitty so that the men could be kept on and paid a retainer, you could be sent to work on any ship for any line. I worked six years as a 'temporary' and then I did nine months probation to see if I was good enough, and then I was taken on as permanent staff."

In 1968 Southampton Harbour Board amalgamated with the British Transport Docks Board, who had taken over ownership of the docks in 1963. With this merger, brought about by the development of con-tainer freight services, came further changes in working conditions for the dockers, when the labour force was decasualised. Every docker now had the same employer and a permanent full-time job. At this time about 1,700 men were registered which rose to around 2,000 with the summer relief temporaries. This figure increased throughout the rest of the 1960s and most of the 1970s.

Ron Williams again describes the work of dockers in the days before containerisation, when goods had to be unloaded manually.

"I started work in the docks in 1954. A lot of the work was seasonal, from April or May to September we worked the fruit boats. The fruit coming from The Cape (South Africa), was handled in the New docks at 101–103 berths, and the outward bound cargoes going to The Cape were loaded in berths 103–105. Cargoes of New Zealand lamb and butter and Argentinian beef used to come to berths 108–109, the international meat store was next to the Graving Dock. The Cape boats used to take a thousand men on a Monday morning and that was to unload the 'homeward', as they called it, the boat that had just come in. That ship would take a week to unload by hand. There might be 10,000 tons of cargo, apples, oranges, eggs, in refrigerated holds. You'd have teams of twelve men loading a hundred boxes onto a cargo board, sending it over by crane to the dockside, and then another team of men unloaded it and put it in sections in the warehouse. Then there was wool to store on the upper storey of the warehouse, and South African gold bars. They were kept in a bullion room on the ship and checked off by the officers and loaded on to railway wagons and sent to the Royal Mint.

"As soon as the cargo was all unloaded the 'load away' began. There were hundreds of lorries and railway waggons taking the goods away to all different parts of the country. Then the whole operation started again to load the ship with export cargo. Everything you can think of was going abroad, textiles, machinery, cars, clothing, it went on round the clock. It was a week's work.

"Today a container can hold 40 tons of goods, and if a container ship comes in at 8 o'clock in the evening it can be unloaded, re-loaded and sail again about eight hours later. It's all done by computerisation and machinery and you hardly need any men to do the job. You hardly see anyone around at a container berth."

The Union Castle Line employed around 750 dockers every day of the year until 1977, when the Cape passenger service ended. These men were divided between the loading and unloading operations and were supplemented by the shore gang, crane-drivers and checkers up to a total of approximately 900. When this freight service was containerised only 170 men were needed. Between 1977 and 1989 the number of dock workers in Southampton fell from over 2,000 down to 670 men. At that point employment was at its lowest ebb, but happily through the 1990s the figure has gradually risen. In 2001 Associated British Ports employs 215 staff directly, including pilots and the back-up launch service. In addition to this figure each of the companies who lease berths and their transit sheds from A.B.P. employs its own staff and dockers, among them Geest (101/2 berth), Canaries Fruit Terminal (103/4), P.&O. (Mayflower Cruise Terminal 105/6), A.&P. (King George V Graving Dock), Amports (201/2), and Southampton Container Terminals Ltd. (203–207). Currently (January 2001) S.C.T. employs 501 staff directly, with 190 contract workers in addition.

When I visited the Container Terminal it certainly seemed strangely deserted, although a huge vessel was in port being unloaded. The human element is missing in the computerised and mechanised port. **Ron Williams** describes his workmates of the 1950s:

"When I was in the docks they were full of real 'characters', it was good to go to work, a pleasure. Arguments could flare up between men one minute, and the next minute they were best mates again, we called it 'Dockology'. When I first went to work in

A container ship unloading at Berth 206. As Ron Williams says, hardly any men are to be seen.
Photograph Peter Wilkinson, 2001.

the docks there was no retirement pension for dockers, they had their Old Age Pension, but nothing extra, and that wasn't enough to live on. There were men of eighty-odd still employed to go and potter around, do a bit of sweeping up or tidying or taking messages, one old boy used to come to work in his slippers. When the pension came in, there was a £100 pay-off scheme, the old fellows would be given the money to retire and take the pension. We younger ones used to say, 'Why don't you take the £100, you silly old b..., and move over and make room for some young ones?'

"The men used to have nicknames for some of the foremen, usually based on some peculiarity or habit. One man was called 'The Balloon', because he would say: 'Don't let me down, lads.' Another was 'The Sheriff', he was always saying: 'Now, what's the hold-up?'

"The docks were the main arteries of Britain at one time. Going to work there was an education, it was a good life, hard work, but very varied. I loved every minute of it."

With all the bustle and noise of ships, cranes, lorries and trains in the container port it is remarkable that sea trout and salmon still make their way up the culverted Tanners Creek and Luggy Creek to spawn in the area between the main terminal road and the railway line. Nature will have its way!

BIBLIOGRAPHY

Moody, Bert: *150 Years of Southampton Docks.*
Williams, David L.: *Docks and Ports: 1 Southampton.*

We would particularly like to thank the following for their kindness in showing us round their premises and explaining the work that goes on there:

Steve Gallagher – *A&P. Southampton Ltd. (King George V Graving Dock).*
Ron Hancock – *Associated British Ports.*
Richard Lewis – *The Geest Line.*
Derek Smith – *Southampton Container Terminals Ltd.*

Luggy Creek, where sea trout and salmon still spawn close to the Freightliner Terminal. The spire of Holy Trinity can be seen in the background. *Photograph Peter Wilkinson.*

CHAPTER XII

Village Life

In the year 2000 Millbrook bears little resemblance to the country village it once was. Within living memory it was a close knit community with an identity of its own. People did the things you expect villagers to have done. They went to church, there were summer fetes and Christmas bazaars, and children played in the fields, watched the village blacksmith, or helped on the farm.

The Parish magazine kept villagers up to date with local events and parochial announcements. In the 1930s, before there was any National Health, the services of a Parish Nurse were available free to all parishioners. In 1936 the scheme was re-organised and a contribution of one halfpenny per week was required for those wishing to participate. The Millbrook Dramatic Society was performing 'Nothing but the Truth' at the Church House in May 1936. At the Christmas Bazaar 16/– was raised by Madame Suzette telling fortunes, £10.8s.0d. by Miss Francis on the Fancy Stall, and 19/5d by Mrs Paul on the Hoop-la stand. The magazine reflects a comfortable and secure way of life, which seems to have disappeared in the 21st century.

I spoke to several people who knew Millbrook when they were children and the village they describe seems to be in a vanished world.

Edna De la Cour, nee Marchant, sets the scene, describing Millbrook as it was in the 1920s and 30s. She wrote down these memories for her grandchildren:

"Millbrook Pond could be described as a country crossroads where Millbrook and Redbridge merged together. Starting at one corner, opposite our house, was the Swan public house, next door was Pondside Farm occupied by the Southwells, then a small meadow, then the pond itself. It was fed by a stream, which ran from the local Rec. through a pipe under the road and into the pond just alongside the smithy's workshop. A small footbridge was built to one side where the stream continued through private property and where beautiful watercress grew.

"Over the bridge was Blacksmith Barnes' forge. It was a thrill to watch this craftsman at work. It was a noisy process, first he would pump the bellows until the embers glowed bright red, there was much clanging as he shaped the shoe on the anvil, then the wonderful sizzling as he plunged it into cold water, steam hissing everywhere. Finally we would hold our breath and wince with fear as the shoe was fitted to the horse's hoof and

Picturesque thatched cottages at the Four Posts end of Millbrook Road. This was known as the Four Posts Mission room. *Southampton City Cultural Services.*

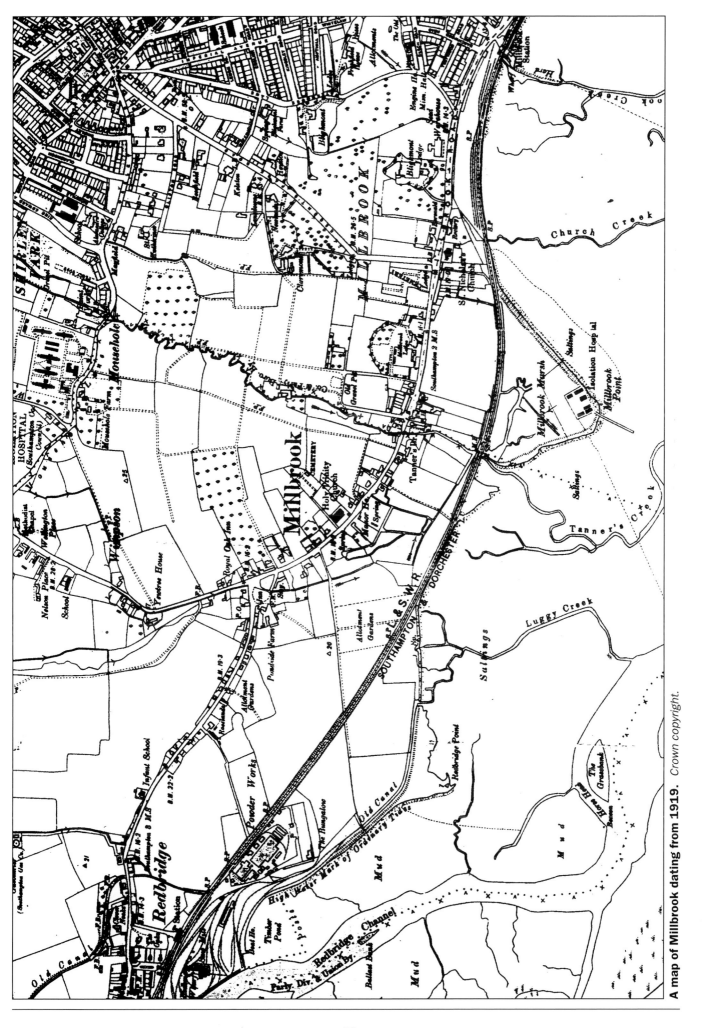

A map of Millbrook dating from 1919. *Crown copyright.*

Redbridge Road, probably early 1900s. The road is curving round towards the pond. The white building on the right is The Swan public house, as indicated by the sign hanging outside. On the wall it says, 'Wines and spirits, fine old Scotch whisky'. If you walked on down this road you would come to the pond as shown in the next photograph.
Photograph courtesy of John Coney.

Millbrook Pond photographed from outside The Swan. The buildings opposite are, left to right, the fish shop, the butcher's, Elliot's cycle shop and garage, and the Adult School.
Photograph courtesy of John Coney.

Millbrook Pond, probably early 1900s. This photograph is taken looking back up Redbridge Road. The Swan is on the left of the picture, the building on the right was the Post Office, which later became a transport café. The little bridge over the piped stream, mentioned by Edna De la Cour, is in the foreground. The bridge also appears in the previous photograph.
Southampton City Cultural Services.

blue smoke and an acrid smell filled the air. Across the main road there was the village Post Office, the darkest and dingiest shop I have ever known. A tinny old bell would jangle as the door was opened. A huge wooden counter ran the length of the shop, on which stood large tins with faded pictures of 'Victory V' gums, Fishermen's Friend lozenges etc. There never appeared to be any daylight in this shop, an old gas lamp glimmered faintly casting eerie shadows. Two spinster sisters, the Misses Carpenter, were the proprietors of this establishment and they looked as if they had stepped out of a Dickens novel. Very thin gold-rimmed half spectacles rested on the tip of the nose of the sister who served behind the Post Office counter. The other lady was tall, thin, gaunt, with a long necklace of large beads adorning her flat chest. Across Wimpson Lane there was a transport café which had quite a large yard to the rear for overnight lorry drivers."

Millbrook, in the first half of the Twentieth Century, was a paradise for children. There was little traffic to worry about, there were streams and fields and woods to play in and the beach to visit.

Jean Barker describes her childhood. She now lives in Maybush Road.

"I was born in Millbrook, in Victory Road, in 1928. When I was little Millbrook was so different, I can hardly recognise it now.

"The railway station was beautiful, there were roses growing up trellis all around the building, it was a lovely little station. Next to the station there was a tall pointed building, like an oast house, where they used to make malt. The pub near the station was called the Railway Hotel and they used to make their own beer. The sea almost came up to the railway line, beyond it there was a low white wall and a pathway and then you were on the beach. It was a shingle beach with a bit of sand. I can remember walking all along the sea wall, holding my father's hand, right as far as a bridge at Four Post Hill. They started draining the bay back and filling it in a few years before the war, suddenly our lovely beach vanished. For years there was a dredger working, it was like an old friend moaning and clanking around. The bay turned into a huge marsh at first, a sort of red, rusty coloured mud, and lots of flowers started to grow in it. Then they left it to dry out and didn't start to build on it properly until after the war.

"In my childhood there were houses all along Millbrook Road, lovely houses, they could look right out over the water. The old Millbrook Church, St. Nicholas', was still there, but it was in a very dilapidated state. We used to play in the churchyard, I used to stand on the big flat tombs and watch the ships coming in. Sometimes we'd play hide and seek round the graves or use the flat tops as picnic tables for our sandwiches. One day we were poking around the edges of a tombstone with a piece of wood and we found we could lever the side off, my dare-devil brother climbed right inside. We were horrified and hid behind the graves until he came out. There was a big empty house next to the church, which we kids used to call the House of the Seven Sisters, because it had seven rooms upstairs and seven rooms downstairs. We used to run in there if it rained and play hide and seek. Then next door to that was a tumble-down place where a lady used to sell home-made sweets in tight little rolls of newspaper. The church was on the opposite side of the road from the graveyard, and a pathway ran beside it down to the beach. We used to go swimming there, we called it 'The Shingle', we could stay there all day waiting for the tide to come in and out. They built a boat-house there and made it into a sailing club. The last time I went down there must be thirty years ago, but I believe it's all gone now.

"Before they built Millbrook roundabout there was a public house called The Swan, and in front of that there was a big pond, we used to go down there catching tadpoles and frogs.

"The road off to Redbridge was very narrow, and there were little houses along it. They were hung with slates over the walls and they were so small that when you opened the front door you went straight into the living room. Then there was a pub called the Oliver Cromwell, it was terribly old and the steps were worn right down into a hollow in the doorway. Of course they were all pulled down for the road improvements. Next to Tanners Brook there was a building like a big shed and an old man lived in there. He made toys out of pieces of wood, all sorts of things, dolls' cradles, bikes, little prams, all brightly painted in reds and yellows and blues. They hung from the ceiling on bits of string, we children thought he was wonderful and he used to let us sit and watch him working on the toys. He was just like Father Christmas.

"Tanners Brook comes out just next to the old St. Nicholas' churchyard. We used to play down there for hours, we made a rope swing from a tree and we paddled in the water too. The stream was so clear and clean you could drink the water.

"I was christened at the Holy Trinity Church in Millbrook, but we went to the Millbrook Union Baptist chapel in Testwood Road, opposite the fish and chip shop. We practically spent our whole lives in that church, I think it was an excuse to get the children out of the house. Every night after school we went to the church for something, Bible reading, or Band of Hope, or Magic Lantern shows. There you were, a little child of six or seven saying, 'I promise to abstain from all intoxicating liquors and to help others to do the same, so help me God.' Nobody ever told you what intoxicating meant, or abstain, you just said it parrot fashion. You just gave your heart to Christ and then you were a good girl. On Sundays we went to church and Sunday school

Some of the old 'characters' of the village outside the Oliver Cromwell pub, probably in the 1920s. 'Old Ned' is seated with the dog on his lap.
Photograph Mrs B. E. Joiner.

three times. The only day we didn't go to church was a Saturday and then we went to the pictures in the afternoon.

"Our house in Victory Road was semi-detached, it was a lovely little area when we were children. The mothers would be outside whitening their doorsteps and polishing the brass doorknockers, keeping it all spick and span. The neighbours were lovely too, we sometimes went on outings in a coach to the seaside, the whole street together. John Stonehouse, the politician, lived in Victory Road when he was a child. Indoors we always had a fire in the kitchen, summer and winter. There was a big copper in the scullery and if you wanted hot water you filled it up and lit a fire underneath it. You had to bale it out into a tin bath in the kitchen for everyone to get washed. My father worked at the power station in town, he was called 'Smiler' because he was always laughing and joking. My parents were very strict with us. They were born in the 1890s, so they were brought up in the Victorian era, and my mother never mentioned anything about sex education. I was seventeen when my elder married sister had a baby, but I had no idea how she got it, and when she came to visit, I had to leave the room while she was feeding it."

No village would be complete without its 'characters', and Millbrook had plenty of those. In the 1920s a Mr Ned Taylor lived at Elm Cottage. He was the local knacker and could often be seen driving his cart through the village with a dead horse on it, the head hanging over one side and the tail over the other. He had a signboard outside his cottage saying, 'Good Oss Oil' (with the ss reversed) and a clock with no hands announcing, 'No tick here' (i.e. no credit). Apparently the 'Oss Oil' was invaluable in the relief of aches and pains, but whether this was for horses or humans is not

clear. There was also a small coffin nailed to his shed, and according to **John Coney** who has collected many anecdotes about the village, the story behind this was as follows: A carpenter's little daughter was ill and not expected to survive so her father made a coffin ready for her. Ned heard about this and was so angry that he went round to the house while the carpenter was out at the pub and took the coffin. He told the father what he thought of him and said he would nail the coffin to his wall, and heaven help anyone who tried to take it down. The story had a happy ending because the child recovered and grew up to have children of her own.

Shopping was a very different experience in the 1920s and '30s before the advent of supermarkets or the existence of strict hygiene regulations. Milk was sold from a horse drawn cart which went round the village, the milk being ladled out into the customer's jug from a churn. Home made ice-cream was sold by 'Old Beardy', a man with an enormous beard, over his garden gate at Gothic cottage, it was said to be more ice than cream.

Ivy Weston's shop in Vulcan Terrace was legendary for selling absolutely everything from groceries to soap, candles, sweets and toys. Children would spend ages agonising over the choice between gobstoppers or

Ivy Weston's shop in Vulcan Terrace. *Southampton City Archives.*

sherbet dips in her shop, whilst housewives lingered for a few minutes gossip. Ivy could be relied upon to know everything about everybody in the village. Mrs Shepherd at the Post Office sold slices of rich plum cake and Mr Legge sold papers and tobacco in his paraffin smelling hut.

There was Bordycott's grocery up near the pond and two baker's shops in Wimpson Lane.

Millbrook was well provided with public houses. There was The Royal Mail just near the bridge over Tanners Brook, it was said to have been a coaching inn. There was a stable next to the pub where the coach horses were changed and the mail used to be handled.

Cricketers used to change at the pub before playing on Millbrook Cricket Club ground, which was behind Vulcan Terrace. The Royal Mail was demolished in 1967. Not far from the Royal Mail was The Oliver Cromwell, yet another pub reckoned to be centuries old. It was opposite Victoria Lodge in Millbrook Road, near Tanners bridge. It is said to have been named after Oliver Cromwell because he stayed the night at the inn, but there is no evidence to prove this.

The Royal Oak stood near the pond, a little way up Wimpson Lane. It was also supposed to be of great age and was greatly regretted when its turn came for demolition in 1972. In the Echo the regulars spoke of the times when the stream used to flood and water came under the door. The whole place would be ankle deep in water and customers came in wearing wellingtons. The new Royal Oak with its fitted carpets would never have the same atmosphere. This pub has in its turn been demolished in recent years and replaced with shops. The Swan stood very near the pond. Its modern replacement was renamed The Fighting Cocks, but that too disappeared when the site was redeveloped as a Macdonalds restaurant in 2000. Further along Millbrook Road, just near the end of Waterhouse Lane, stood The Sailor's Return, whose first landlord is recorded as opening for business in 1869. This pub was demolished in 2001. The Bricklayers Arms in Wimpson Lane dates from 1819 when Sir Charles Mill leased the premises to David Tubb. In 1859 a street directory listed George Brackstone as the licensee. It must have originally catered for labourers in the nearby brickfields, and it is still a popular hostelry.

Barry Ross is a retired builder who now lives in the New Forest. He remembers Millbrook in the 1920s and early '30s.

"We lived almost opposite the Oliver Cromwell public house. It's difficult to imagine if you've only

The Oliver Cromwell pub. *Southampton City Archives.*

ever known Millbrook Road as it is now, but it used to be just an ordinary narrow road with houses close to the pavement, like the service road is in front of Holy Trinity Church.

"Millbrook was very rural then, once you got over Tanners Brook you were in the country. The new dual carriageway was built next to the old Millbrook Road and went over the site of most of the old buildings.

"Our house wasn't a cottage, it was a big Victorian house called Victoria Lodge. It had an acre of ground with a six-foot high brick wall all the way around it. The rooms had high ceilings with cornices, it was quite grand. It had a front staircase and back stairs for the servants, with servants' quarters at the rear of the house. I only had two sisters and I think there were at least five main bedrooms, so a lot of the rooms weren't occupied at all. We didn't have servants ourselves, Mother ran the house, but a

The Bricklayers Arms in the early 1900s.
Photograph courtesy of Jane Jamieson.

Cottages next to Tanners Brook, early 1900s.
Photographed by E. Philipps, reproduced by kind permission of Jennifer Robinson.

woman came in every day to help her. The gardens were beautiful. There was a large lawn, a vegetable garden and tons of fruit trees. The summerhouse was covered with climbing loganberries. My father was a very keen gardener, and then, as we grew up, we all had to do something to help, weeding and tidying. We didn't have a gardener as such, but if there wasn't much building work for the men to do they would come and do a few jobs around the garden too. You see my father was a builder and he took over the business of Pitt's the builders who operated from Victoria Lodge. There were offices and stores within the grounds. We left there in the early 1930s. We never owned the house, it was rented on a lease, and when it expired we weren't able to renew it. Obviously that was because of the road building plans.

"When I went back recently, I parked in the service road outside the church and it was so hard to believe that this was the main road, now it seems like nothing, just a little side-road. You look across to the east-bound carriageway and the west bound carriageway and all this traffic thundering along and it's very hard to visualise what it used to be like. When you went along that road towards Totton, about a quarter of a mile past the church, you came to a junction by the village pond. If you turned left, the road took you round to the causeway, that little narrow, grey-stone bridge, and over the river. That was the only road out of Southampton going to the New Forest and Bournemouth. If you turned right, that was Wimpson Lane leading to farmland. There was no traffic to speak of.

"I started school at Freemantle but after a year or two I went to Hurst Leigh School in the Polygon, so I didn't play with the local children much. My school friends would come to play in our enormous garden and we had our own gang of naughty boys inside the

garden walls. I used to cycle to school, and in the winter, by the time we came home it was pitch dark, and there were no street lights once you got to Tanners Brook. That was the country.

"The road surface changed at that point as well, beyond the boundary of Southampton it was only gravelled. This was in the 1920s. I never used to play on the sea-shore myself, but I remember when they started reclaiming the land for the docks because there was the noise of the pile drivers going on day and night.

"Between our house and the church there was a market garden owned by the Marchants. I don't know what they used to grow in the gardens, you don't notice things like that when you're young, but

A Southampton Corporation Tramways bus at the Tanners Brook stop in 1919. The signboard on the side of the bus reads 'Floating bridge, Tanners Brook, West Station (i.e. Southampton Central), Millbrook Road.' *From the collection of Bert Moody.*

I do remember that they did all the work on the land with horses, ploughing and so on. There was quite a sensation in the village once when one of the farm workers got kicked full in the face by a horse, he was in a very bad way. He forgot the rule that you shouldn't stand behind a horse. He recovered, but it was the talk of Millbrook for a while.

"We went to church at Holy Trinity. The old church at the bottom of Regents Park Road was already partly derelict. Holy Trinity was very High Church, incense and so on. We had to go to services all dressed up in our Sunday best, but as we got older and weren't made to go, we drifted away.

"When you're young you don't take much notice of your surroundings, I know there were other big houses near us but I've no idea who lived in them. We got to know the Bromleys who ran the White House Garage at the bottom of Regents Park Road. They had a garage and bicycle repair shop in Shirley Road, Dowding and Bromley, and they opened up this other branch in Millbrook. There were no self-service pumps in those days, the attendant had to wind a handle round to pump the petrol up. They did motor repairs and also bicycle repairs, especially punctures, which were a big thing with the poor road surfaces. Before the War, cars were pretty thin on the ground so the motor side of the business wouldn't have been enough to keep them going. When I was a boy, in the 1920s, it was still quite an event to see cars coming along Millbrook Road. Motoring was a real joy then.

"As kids, we used to go in Mrs Weston's sweet shop. She sold those old fashioned things like gob-stoppers, liquorice bootlaces, sherbet dips, you name it, she had it. I think she just catered for the children, she didn't have anything of quality in there. My sisters or my friends and I would go in there to spend our pocket money. The Royal Mail pub also had a little sweet shop attached to it and we sometimes went in there for penny bars of chocolate. If you had sixpence [equivalent to two and a half pence] in those days it was really worth something, and you could buy all sorts of sweets. We felt as if we were doing all the shopkeepers a good turn by spending our money and we'd spend ages trying to decide what to have. It was a case of, 'Mm, no I don't think so, I'll try over the road at the Royal Mail, thank you.' Mrs Weston was better for sherbet dabs anyway.

"Another place I used to go was Mr. Legge's paper shop. It was just an old wooden hut really and he only sold newspapers and tobacco. Winter and summer alike he had a Valor oil stove going. You can imagine the heat in that little hut, and the smell! Modern paraffin stoves hardly smell at all, but that old Valor stove stank. My father smoked and he quite often asked me to go over there to get him tobacco or a paper, so I got to know Mr Legge. I used to get my comics there – *Tiger Tim*, *Gem*, *Bubbles* and *Nelson Leigh*, that was a school one, all about

the Upper Fifth Form and schoolboy adventures. Mr Legge was a real character and he was a bit disabled.

"In those days tons of people who lived out that way, even in Totton, worked in Southampton. They all used bicycles to get to work and went by his hut. What could be more convenient? They could just stop and go in for their fags or a paper, so he did a roaring trade. He knew what he was doing when he went there to set up a business.

"In those days we were the only people in the village who had the telephone, it was quite something to have one, but of course Father needed it for the business. People would often come in and ask to use our 'phone for some urgent message such as sending for the doctor, and also we'd get people 'phoning up and saying things like, 'You live opposite Mrs. Smith, don't you? Well, could you run across and tell her that Jim's ill.'

"I don't remember there being a doctor in Millbrook at all, they were fairly thin on the ground anyway in the '20s. If we were ill the doctor came from Shirley.

"When I was a boy, Regents Park Road wasn't built up at all, there were just a few individual big houses among fields and market gardens and the road itself was more or less a track. Then as the houses became dilapidated they were just pulled down and three or four new houses built on the site, so it was developed in the years shortly before the War.

"When I look at Millbrook today, even though I can remember it, I wonder if I'm right about things, it looks so totally different. There are hardly any landmarks left to work out where places were, except Tanners Brook and the church. When I drive past I really can't visualise how it used to be."

John Northcott now lives in Bitterne, but in the 1930s he too was a Millbrook boy.

"When I lived in Regents Park Road, down at the bottom end below Claremont Crescent, it was very nearly the western boundary of Southampton. I think Tanners Brook was the actual boundary. There were just fields to the west of that. King George's Avenue was partly built, but it was developed piece-meal, when a builder got a bit of money together he would build a few more houses, and so on.

"Behind our house in Regents Park Road was a quarter acre patch where they used to grow flowers, it was just the place to go for me to buy flowers for my mother on Mothering Sunday. As children we used to play all round Tanners Brook or at a place called The Flood, which was near the shore during the construction of the Graving Dock.

"We had rafts and planks to play on, all strictly forbidden of course. When you went over the railway level crossing there was a group of huts which was an Isolation Hospital, built to replace the old ship that served as a Quarantine hospital for years.

Bathers at Millbrook shore 1916. In the background is the shed of Woodcock's boatyard. *Photographed by E. Philipps, reproduced by kind permission of Jennifer Robinson.*

"The sea used to come right up near the railway line before all the land was reclaimed; in fact the Central Station used to get flooded sometimes. We used to go swimming off Millbrook Point, it had a shingle beach, and there was also Millbrook Sailing Club in the bay. My Grandfather was in the Coast guard over in Marchwood and his daughters, my aunts, used to take the Penny Ferry across the water from Marchwood to Millbrook Point.

"We also played in the fields and lanes. Our territory stretched from Barter's Farm, which is where Tesco's filling station is now, down to Millbrook and across to Nursling. There was a foot-path from Barter's Farm which ran right down as far as Millbrook Road, to a little smithy next to the pond. There were several Market Gardens in the area growing fruit and vegetables for sale in Southampton.

"You mustn't imagine that Millbrook was completely rural. Behind where the shops are at the bottom of King George's Avenue now, there used to be a scrap-yard owned by someone called Mr. Axton, and it was full of bits of old ships, funnels, anchors, that sort of thing. There was also a British Oxygen factory, and the Tobacco factory. So it wasn't all beautiful countryside around Millbrook."

John Northcott mentions the Quarantine Hospital-Ship off Millbrook Point and this seems an appropriate point to include information about the 'Floating Fever Isolation Sanatorium', as it was officially called.

In the days before antibiotics, infectious diseases were a serious threat to the population, and Southampton

The Floating Fever Isolation Sanatorium, *City of Adelaide,* **photographed by L. A. Pritchard.**
From the collection of Bert Moody.

was particularly at risk because of the large number of ships using the port. Due to increasing numbers of sailors returning to the town from abroad with small-pox and other dangerous infections, Southampton Corporation decided to acquire a large ship to use as a Port Sanatorium. In 1893 the Port Authority purch-ased a vessel called *City of Adelaide*. This ship had been built in 1864 and worked as a passenger liner to Australia. In her new role as an isolation unit, she was anchored off Millbrook Point in the River Test, away from yachts and shipping lanes.

The vessel was in a poor condition and major refurbishment was necessary before it could be used as a hospital. Three wards were constructed, along with an administrative section and a promenade deck. The Annual Report on the Health of the County Borough of Southampton records the numbers of smallpox cases admitted to the Floating Hospital: 1894 – 4 cases, 1895 – 4 cases, 1896 – 11 cases, 1897 – 15 cases, 1899 – 12 cases, 1900 – 19 cases.

In 1924 it was judged that the ship was no longer adequate and it was replaced by the Millbrook Marsh Isolation Hospital. *City of Adelaide* was sold, re-named *Carrick*, and became the home of a Royal Naval Volunteer Reserve club at Glasgow.

The new smallpox hospital was situated at Millbrook Marsh, just near where the ship had been moored, on a 21 acre plot of land, bounded on two sides by Southampton Water and on the third side by the railway line. Accommodation was in three wooden military huts. In 1929 the Medical Officer of Health, Dr R. E. Lander stated:

"The Port of Southampton being in direct communi-cation with almost all countries in the world, runs considerable danger of the importation of infectious diseases and many vessels arrive from ports which are infected with cholera, yellow fever, smallpox or plague. All cases of acute infectious diseases are removed by motor ambulance to Southampton Isolation Hospital. Smallpox cases are removed to the smallpox huts at Millbrook Marsh."

It is not clear exactly when the Millbrook Marsh Hospital closed down, but certainly by the 1930s the incidence of smallpox had been greatly reduced by vaccination programmes. It seems likely that the hos-pital closed down when work started on reclaiming land in the area.

Infectious diseases were still very much of a threat in the early 1920s and apart from the Millbrook Marsh unit, there was also an Isolation Hospital in Oakley Road. This hospital consisted of various separate wards in pavilions and took mainly cases of tuber-culosis, and other more common serious infections. In 1924 a total of 778 cases were admitted, suffering from illnesses such as scarlet fever, diphtheria, tuberculosis, cerebro-spinal fever, and measles. In 1944 the Health Authorities purchased and adapted several military huts, which had been built on the site during the war,

and created new isolation cubicles. The hospital later became the Chest Hospital, specialising in lung and heart problems. When that department was trans-ferred to the Southampton General Hospital, the site was sold to Tesco for a superstore, except for an area reserved for a Community Hospital for the elderly, the Western Hospital.

Dennis Mills was a boy living in Millbrook in the late 1920s. He is able to shed more light on the Sailing Club and the shore:

"We went to live in Millbrook Road in 1928. We had a house near the Sailor's Return public house, just opposite the station and the station master's house. The tram terminal was nearly outside our house. It was quite a little self-contained community round there, we had several corner shops selling everything you needed, groceries, papers, a green-grocer and a fish and chip shop. There was even a man who went round every morning selling fresh fish from a donkey and cart.

"The railway line used to go all along the Millbrook shore and Woodcock's boatyard and a sailing club were opposite the station. There was a slipway and hard and a big boathouse, which was in the yard, and next to that there was a sort of swimming pool which we called 'The Flood'. Going back before my time there used to be a ferry across from Millbrook shore to Marchwood, a man with a rowing boat would take people across for a few pence. You could get across the railway line to the boatyard and sailing club and the beach by a level crossing, then later on they built a pedestrian bridge over the line. This shingle beach went right as far as the Central Station and it was very popular with the locals in the summertime. Loads of people went there on a sunny day, there was everything you could want, the beach, swimming, boats to hire, ice cream for sale, we could even do a bit of train spotting and wait for the Bournemouth Belle to go past twice a day.

"As a boy I helped out at Woodcock's boatyard, I got paid sixpence a week. They used to have five skiffs, rowing boats, which people could hire for the afternoon in the summer, and at the end of the day my friend and I had the job of towing them out to their mooring. Sometimes we ferried people out to their yachts in a little flat-bottomed dinghy and they'd give us a penny or two. They weren't grand yachts like you see today, just eighteen to twenty footers, and they belonged to local people from Millbrook and Shirley. Mr Toogood's son, the seed merchants, he had a nice speed boat there. My grandfather was a great one for sailing, he had two boats, sometimes we went out sailing with him, but quite often he had us scrubbing the bottom or painting something instead. In the 1930s Millbrook sailing club held a regatta every summer. There would be sailing dinghy races down to the Royal Pier and four-man rowing boat races. Other rowing clubs

The Manor house. This stood opposite Holy Trinity church.
Photograph courtesy of Jim Hann

like the Coalporters' Club would come and compete. They used to have a bigger yacht done up as a pirate ship with a 'Jolly Roger' flag and sailors in fancy dress and boys would go out in rowing boats and attack it and try to capture the flag, it was great fun. I learned to sail by myself when I was nine, and I learned to swim down there. Some men used to dig rag-worms in the mud at low tide, to sell to fishermen, and I used to help with that too. You could catch plaice, flounders, whiting, eels, you could always reckon on catching something.

"When they started work on the New Docks, the Sailing Club was turned out of the Millbrook shore and had to go up to Millbrook Point. We had a club house there, but the boatyard closed down.

"When they started reclaiming the land for the New Docks, they blocked it off first of all with concrete caissons from the Mayflower Park end and made a wide bank and began to pump out the water. They were dredging an 80-foot deep channel for the liners, and they dumped all that silt into the landfill site. The soil that was dug out for the Graving Dock was also put in there, they had a little train which carried the spoil along. After a couple of years it was full, but then it had to be left to settle and dry out and get hard. Shrubs and plants grew on the land. When King George V opened the Graving Dock we sat up in my grandmother's front bedroom, a neighbour lent us a telescope, and we saw the royal yacht sail in and the King and Queen coming down the gangway."

Ellen Hann (nee Southwell), who likes to be called Nellie, was born at Swan Cottages in Millbrook in 1922. As a young girl she worked 'in service' at The Manor House. This house was reputed to be Sixteenth

Century in origin but with later additions and alterations. Going into service as a domestic worker was one of the few jobs open to young women until well after the First World War, but today hardly any girls would consider this as a career option. Her memories make fascinating and revealing reading:

"My Mum and Dad worked at the Manor House, so we 'lived in'. The house stood opposite Holy Trinity church and it was right by the water in those days, there was marshy land at the bottom of the grounds. It was a lovely house, very old, it had a wonderful staircase, but it was full of rats. There was a huge stone-flagged kitchen with a water pump, and you might be sitting in there quietly in the evening and rats would run along the big pipes on the walls. I wasn't scared of them at all, I just used to stamp my feet to scare them away. They would be lurking on the back stairs, along the corridors, and there was always one in the dairy.

"There was a tunnel under the kitchen floor, which was blocked off in my time, and it was supposed to lead down to the waterfront. If you were sitting in the kitchen when the tide came in you could hear the swishing of the water and a clanking sound like chains. People said the rattling noise was from chains which had been put there for mooring boats inside the tunnel. In the village it was believed that it was a secret passageway used by smugglers, but nobody really knew why it was built. There's still a ventilation shaft for the tunnel in the grounds of Holy Trinity, but it doesn't go anywhere now. The tunnel disappeared when the Manor House was demolished, so we'll never know for sure.

"The Manor House was a boarding house in the 1920s and '30s, genteel people lived there, people with plenty of money who sometimes went on winter cruises, real gentry. There were eight or nine boarders. It was owned by a Miss Bond and her sister, Mrs. Stubbs. I believe they bought the house from the Barker-Mill estate. They gave up the boarding house at the beginning of the War and the army took it over. Miss Bond worked very hard, she did all the cooking. There were three gentlemen boarders who came from London and were working locally. Nelson Keyes, the actor, lived there, and two town councillors, Mr. Mansel and Mrs. Riley. They hated each other, and they're buried side by side in the churchyard now.

"My father looked after the farm at the Manor House. There were chickens and ducks and three cows kept specially to supply the boarders. He grew all the vegetables and fruit for the table, there was a huge kitchen garden and orchard in the grounds. We used to make our own butter, churn it by hand and then make it into pats. The cows supplied all our milk and cream.

"When I left school at fourteen I went into service there. I did everything. I had to start work at six o'clock. My first job was to clean out all the grates and lay the fires, I put paper and sticks and coal in the grate. The dining room fire and the drawing room fire had to be lit before anyone came down, and I had to keep them going with fresh coal all day. The steps up to the front door had to be scrubbed and rubbed with white hearthstone every morning and the brass knocker had to be polished with Brasso. We had a day for cleaning all the silver every week, not only the knives and forks but the ornaments too. We had wooden carpet sweepers which picked up the crumbs, but at spring-cleaning time we took the carpets out into the yard and hung them over the washing line and hit them with a carpet beater to get out all the dust and grit. The boarders sent their personal washing out to a laundry but we had to wash the sheets and bedclothes. There was a wash-house in the yard and we boiled the sheets in a big copper with a fire underneath it. They were cotton sheets, so they had to be ironed as well.

"In the morning I had to take up big jugs of hot water for people to get washed, there wasn't any running hot water. Then I had to take out the 'slops', there weren't any flush toilets so all the boarders had a commode with a bucket inside it which had to be emptied. Miss Bond did eventually have a proper bathroom put in with a bath and toilet, so that was a big improvement. The boarders always had a tray of tea in the morning, not just a cup of tea, with nice china. Breakfast was at nine o'clock, bacon and eggs and so on, and we had to serve them. There was a lovely white damask tablecloth and serviettes, none of these paper napkins! We had beautiful china and silverware and the table was always set with all the correct cutlery and glasses for every meal. Lunch was at one o'clock and afternoon tea at four. The boarders spent their days sitting in the drawing

room, reading and chatting, or they would take a stroll round the garden. We weren't allowed in the garden when they were there. Dinner was served at seven o'clock. There would be huge joints of beef, or pork, or chicken from our own farm, and all the homegrown vegetables, it was lovely food. I didn't do much cooking but I had to help with preparing vegetables, and I used to 'pull' chickens, clean out all the insides and pluck the feathers.

When I think about it, I really did work very hard."

One of the boarders that Mrs.Hann mentions was Owen Llewellyn Mansel. He was the son of a Dorset vicar and a cousin of Lord Radstock of Mayfield House over at Weston in Southampton. Mr. Mansel devoted much of his time and energy to public service and from 1919–30 he was a member of the Millbrook parish council and the Board of Guardians. A tribute paid to him in 1931 said that he had laboured strenuously in the interests of the parish and accomplished a great deal of good work. He campaigned to get the first council houses built at Wimpson in 1926, saying that the old cottages were "not decent for the twentieth century." He pressed for better facilities at Wimpson and Redbridge schools and also urged that Millbrook should join Southampton, rather than Romsey and Stockbridge. After his death in 1931 the lane between Wimpson and Upper Wimpson farms was named Mansel Road in his honour. (More Stories of Southampton Streets, A. G. K. Leonard.)

Schoolboy stories about the Manor House claimed that there was an underground tunnel, leading from the house to the waterfront, which was used by smugglers. Sometimes such stories have a basis in fact, but despite checking through Admiralty Court records I could find no evidence to suggest that the seafarers of Millbrook did anything worse that sell oysters illicitly. Old maps provided no clues to the existence of a tunnel, but did show that in 1801 the Southampton to Salisbury canal was cut between the site of the Manor House and the shore, making it impossible for any tunnel to have a connection with the sea.

However, there was still Nellie Hann's intriguing information that you could hear the sound of swishing water and clanking chains in the kitchen of the Manor House when the tide came in. Local legend said that this was caused by mooring chains for boats inside the tunnel clanking as the tide flooded over them. This was clearly impossible, but there had to be some explanation for this strange phenomenon.

I consulted Geologist and Geotechnical Engineer, Terry Rickeard B.SC., M.SC., F.G.S. and he readily supplied the probable, and rather less romantic, answer:

"The underlying soil of Millbrook is a porous gravel through which ground water gradually drains towards the sea, the Test estuary in this case. When the tide comes in it causes pressure against the water which is draining out and makes it 'back up'. This effect is felt as much as a quarter of a mile inland from the sea, and is shown by a rise in the level of water in streams and ditches. The tunnel under the floor of the Manor House was a well, as the pump in the corner of the kitchen indicates. This must have been fed by an underground spring, which would have been affected by the flow of the tides and caused the level of the water in the well to fluctuate. This would account for the sound of swishing water. There was probably an old chain for a well bucket hanging down into the water and, as the level rose and fell, it clanked around."

Another familiar figure around the village would have been the coalman. Although people still do have open fires, they are very much in the minority since the Clean Air Act and the increasing popularity of central heating, and the coalman is something of a rarity.

Peter Lisle was a coalman in the 1960s and served the new Council Estate as well as older parts of Millbrook. He wrote down his memories of his working days:

"I left school in 1945 and went to work for the Ordnance Survey in Chessington. Then I went in the army for two years National Service, so I was away from the area for four years altogether. I came back in December 1949 and the building of the Millbrook housing estate was at its height. I went for a walk over the same land as we walked to school and got lost.

"I went to work at the Ordnance Survey in Southampton and occasionally helped my father in his coal business when he was particularly busy. In 1962 he decided to retire and offered me the business if I wanted it. I was thirty-one at the time. It was a big decision to make, but in the Civil Service, although there are many benefits, I knew that I would be doing the same at sixty as I was at thirty, so I decided to have a try at being a coal merchant.

"It was a far different business when I retired than it was in 1962. Most houses still had coal fires, but by the time I finished nearly everybody had gone over to gas and electricity and there was not a lot of trade left. In the winter of 1962–3, which was very severe, I needed forty-eight hour days because there was such demand for coal. That winter the snow started on Boxing Day 1962 and it froze until the end of February. It's the only time I've ever seen the river freeze over. At low tide when the water was nearly fresh and still, ice formed under the bridge. It was broken up and melted when the tide turned and seawater moved up stream.

"In the sixties, four days a week I made deliveries on Millbrook Estate. In the early years I used to employ a couple of young chaps to help in the winter, also some part-time help, including my 'retired' father. Over the years the trade diminished bit by bit, and when I retired I could do my whole week's work in about two days.

"I had the coal delivered in railway trucks to Millbrook goods yard opposite Blighmont Barracks, there's a Freightliner container terminal there now. The coal was brought in by ship to the wholesaler's wharf at Northam, loaded into railway trucks holding about twelve tons and brought to Millbrook by train. There were other coal merchants who used Millbrook for coal, Sibleys, Lenden's, Co-op, and Edmund Gerald. You backed the lorry on to the truck, let down the opening flap and shovelled coal into the sacks and weighed them on the spot. My father and I could shovel and weigh just over three tons an hour. I had a store at Redbridge in an old building near The Anchor pub, but I never had a yard where I could keep large quantities of fuel. In July 1967 the goods yard at Millbrook was closed and the container depot was built and then I had to go to the wharf at Northam to pick up the coal. By 1986 the coal trade was not very good and the wholesaler sold off part of their wharf and moved to Totton, which was very convenient for me. I finally retired from the coal trade in 1989."

Since the Iron Age, the land of Millbrook has been used for agriculture. Due to the types of soil, which were not particularly rich or fertile, early farms were scattered across the area at roughly half-mile intervals, and this pattern persisted right until modern times. Names which come down from the 19th century, or even earlier, include Bargain Farm, Upper Wimpson Farm, Wimpson Farm, Crabwood Farm, Mousehole Farm, Newlands Farm, Pondside Farm, and Blighmont Farm. In addition there were numerous unnamed market gardens and smallholdings.

I have studied various old maps and it seems that Wimpson Farm was on the area of land enclosed by Evenlode Road, Derwent Road and Mansel Road East, and Upper Wimpson Farm was roughly on the site of the Holy Family School. Newlands Farm was where

Pondside Farm. *Photographed, possibly in the 1930s, by G. E. C. Webb.*

Newlands School stands, with a few large trees from Pickles Copse still remaining in the playing field. Crabwood Farm was in the area enclosed by Thirlmere, Ennerdale, Crabwood and Maybush Roads. Mansel Park was woodland. Mousehole Farm was off Oakley Road opposite Tesco's, and Blighmont Farm was on land next to Waterhouse Lane, now occupied by the B.A.T. factory. Pondside Farm stood next to Millbrook roundabout, and a very large poplar tree, which was near the farmhouse, still stands on a traffic island at the entrance to First Avenue.

These farms are just a memory now, they disappeared beneath housing and roads in the 1950s, but a few people still remember a childhood spent in farming in Millbrook. The names Southwell, Marchant and Hurst have long been associated with the Millbrook area and I was fortunate to be able to talk to members of these old families about their lives.

Ellen 'Nellie' Hann, whose young days 'in service' at the Manor House are described earlier in the chapter, came from the Southwell family who have farmed in the area for generations.

"I was Nellie Southwell before I was married. I was born in 1922 at Swan Cottages in Millbrook, a tree that was in our garden is still growing on the Millbrook roundabout. I never lived on a farm, but most of my relatives were farmers.

Uncle Sid's farm used to stand up a long pathway off Wimpson Lane, his land stretched almost up to Green Lane. I remember the farmhouse was rather ugly, just a square, Victorian sort of house. Uncle Andrew's farm was down by the pond, and that was a pretty farmhouse, small and quaint. In the 1920s and '30s if you went down Regents Park Road, from about Stanton Road onwards, all you could see were fields. Uncle Sid's farm was just agricultural, he grew corn and vegetables, cabbages and potatoes, he didn't have any livestock, but Uncle Andrew had animals. There was also Southwell's Dairy, but they were a more distant branch of the family and we didn't really know them.

"My uncles both worked the land by themselves without any farm labourers. They weren't rich farmers, they couldn't afford tractors. They used horses for some of the farm work, and Uncle Sid had a machine that he walked behind to turn the soil, a cultivator. They worked from daylight to dark, just scratching a living. They both kept chickens, but then everybody kept chickens. When my Mum moved into a small cottage near the pond she still had her chicken run in the garden, and some ducks. Uncle Andrew had pigs. A lot of people in those days had poultry, or a pig fattening up in the back garden. If you look in the doorway of Holy Trinity Church in Millbrook you can see a grille door, that was to keep the animals out. The main door could be left open and this grille was pulled across to prevent any stray cows or sheep from coming in. There were animals grazing all around the church in the fields. There weren't many cars passing by, so it didn't matter if a cow happened to wander across the road."

The Marchants were noted market gardeners in Millbrook. **Edna De la Cour** now lives in Totton, but as a girl she was brought up on the family small-holding. When plans were announced for the construction of the Council Estate and the compulsory purchase of farm land, Edna's father decided to look for a new property before he was forced to leave. He found suitable land out at Botley and continued to farm there until his retirement. Edna's brother is still a farmer, but in Scotland.

"I was born Edna Annie Marchant at Elm Farm, next door to Millbrook Church. When I was two years old we moved to Ettwell House, which was in Redbridge Road very close to the old Millbrook Pond. The property was owned by my great-grandfather, Benjamin George Heath. I always felt that our house was special, with its own front garden and elegant iron railings. The brass door knob was polished and the step whitened every Saturday morning. The kitchen was our living room and the heart of the dwelling. My earliest recollections of this room are lino on the floor with a rag mat in front of the old black range; over this was a mantel piece, a shelf from which hung a strip of brown chenille with dangling tassels. In the middle of the room was a scrubbed wooden table, there was a black horsehair chaise-longue, brown wooden folding shutters at the window, and a gas lamp in the middle of the ceiling. I have treasured memories of making toast on winter evenings in front of the range, and Friday night baths in a tin bath in front of the fire.

"At the rear of the house was a yard, and a pathway which led round a corner to the privy. On the other side of the yard was the stable for our beloved old cart-horse, Dolly, later to be replaced by look-alike Nigger. Then there was a store for the cart and supplies and a shed containing the chaff cutter. Loose hay was fed into it, a wheel was turned by hand and a razor sharp blade cut the hay into short lengths for the horse to eat. The smell of the sweet ripe hay was intoxicating. At the back of the yard was a row of pigsties and a vegetable plot. Beyond this was an acre of arable ground where Dad grew vegetables and flowers. I spent many happy hours as a small child, watching Dad dig the soil, preparing the plot for his seedlings.

"In the top corner of Dad's ground Mrs. Robinson lived in a caravan, quite a remarkable old lady with snowy white hair. She owned a large tricycle on which she pedalled to Bournemouth to visit her sister. Close by her caravan there was a hole in the hedge which divided Dad's property from the Recreation ground, Green Park. We would crawl through it on all fours, dragging dolls' prams, stools, books etc. behind us. The biggest attraction in the 'Rec' was the little stream running down towards Wimpson Lane. This was a favourite place for catching tiddlers and collecting watercress.

Bert Marchant working in his fields with Dolly, 1920s.
Photograph by kind permission of Edna De la Cour.

"Mum kept and bred rabbits, mainly for the butcher's shelf and our own consumption, and it was usually our job to collect their favourite greenery. At this time the only transport Dad had was his old carrier bike and his horse and cart which he used for delivering or collecting supplies at the wholesalers, or trips to farmers in the New Forest area, buying or selling piglets. It was a special treat for my sister Mary and I to be included on these jaunts and if we were especially good Dad would allow us to take turns in holding the reins.

"As well as the land around Ettwell House, Dad farmed a small market garden of about two acres in Gover Road, Redbridge. Mum and Dad toiled for many hours on this plot. When Mary and I were at school we had instructions either to go straight home or down to Redbridge when lessons finished. We quickly got fed up of waiting for Mum and Dad to finish work, so we would wander off to see how many different wild flowers we could find, my favourites being vetch, golden slippers and wild pansies. Often we would lie on our backs in the rhubarb bed trying to focus on the skylarks which were always singing overhead. To break our boredom and to make sure we did our share of work, Mum would get us to count the bundles of whichever produce she was gathering, rhubarb, spring onions, carrots, radishes etc., placing them in piles of twelve. It was always a joy when we could tell her she had reached her target and it was time to load up the cart for the homeward journey. Dad's job it was to cut marrows, cabbages and cauliflowers, or prepare the soil and sow seed.

"I have never known any other woman who worked so long and physically hard as my mother. Mum was always busy helping Dad outdoors on the farm. Saturday was their busiest day of the week.

Starting at daybreak, Dad would load the cart with all the vegetables, salads and flowers he could produce, plus boxes of fruit from the wholesalers. Old Dolly would be harnessed up between the shafts, and the last thing to go aboard was her nosebag of freshly chaffed hay. Taking some packed lunch for themselves, Mum and Dad would set off on a very strenuous day serving customers along Millbrook Road, King George's Avenue, Regents Park, Fawley Road, Blighmont Crescent and Waterhouse Lane. On a good day they would get home by 5 o'clock, and then it was time to start work again feeding all the pigs, chickens and rabbits.

"Because my parents were always very hard working they had very little time to spend on leisure activities with their children, so the meagre number of outings we did embark upon, humble indeed by today's standards, are clearly etched on my memory.

"On today's standards Dad's machinery was quite antiquated. He would harness up old Dolly to the two-shear plough and away he would go, holding the handles steady with his strong arms. It was fascinating to see the shears cutting into and turning over the rich brown soil, burying the surface layer of farmyard manure, and those beautiful straight furrows and perfect spacing of seed rows were proof of his pride in his work.

"Opposite our house in Redbridge Road was a very small shop, which was run by Mr Bordycott who lived in Oakley Road, Shirley. Mum would give him a weekly order and it was Dad's job to collect it on Saturday afternoon. Our order was never ready, and Mary and I would get impatient watching the weekly ritual. Lumps of butter and lard were cut from huge blocks on a marble shelf, blue bags filled with sugar and weighed, wedges of cheese cut with a long wire with a little handle at either end. If there was an occasion during the week when Mum sent us to the shop on our own, it wasn't unusual to be kept waiting for over an hour because we were completely ignored until there was a break in adult customers.

"At a very early age Mary and I were entrusted with the job of delivering a selection of vegetables, specially chosen for their superb quality, to Millbrook Church on the morning of Harvest Festival. Our large dolls' prams were crammed full and we had special instructions not to spill any of the contents.

"My grandfather, Sidney Hurst, was vaguely present in my early life. He was said to be 'The best market gardener in the 'ole of 'ampshire.' Unfortunately he liked a few drinks at the local pub, the Royal Oak. He would go to the pub in his pony and trap and at the end of the evening the landlord would sit him back in the trap and the old nag always found his own way home! He and his wife, Petronella, had a family of twelve children, born between 1903 and 1933. They lived at Claypits Farm cottages, near the brook at Millbrook. Their next door neighbours, the

Bargain Farm, which dates from the late 1400s, photographed in 2000. *Rosaleen Wilkinson.*

historical interest. The thatched farmhouse has a three bay timber frame with wattle and daub infill panels, which are still visible inside the house. Some of the wattle panels have been replaced by bricks and two walls have a complete brick veneer which hides the timber framework, but the structure can still be seen clearly indoors. There are three rooms downstairs, matched by three rooms upstairs, and an extended section next to the kitchen which housed the pantry, dairy, and a storeroom. There are hearths and chimneys in the kitchen and parlour. Keith Dawe, who surveyed the house for the Listing application, considers that the house is late 15th century and is largely unchanged since it was first built. Many of the cottages and farmhouses which once stood in Millbrook must have looked like this house.

Bargain Farm is still a working farm, albeit on a greatly reduced scale from the past, and Mr. Hurst and his sons sell fresh produce from a small farm shop on the premises. However, the green fields which once surrounded the farm are rapidly disappearing under suburban encroachment and the rural view is now dominated by a tennis and sports complex.

Ralph Hurst describes life on the farm.

"My grandfather came from Millbrook originally, he was in farming in the village. After a few years he moved out to a cottage with some land in Brownhill Road, and then in the early 1930s Grandfather finally got the tenancy here at Bargain Farm. The land is owned by the Barker-Mill family. He'd only had the tenancy a couple of years when he died, so my father took over the farm in 1937. I was one year old then and I've lived here nearly all my life. When I got married I moved away and my wife and I had a cottage in Nursling for about eight years. As he got older Dad became ill and couldn't manage, so we came back here to live in 1976, the year of the drought. I didn't have much option, there was nobody else to take on the farm.

Jewels, were also a large family and the two mothers always attended and assisted each other in childbirth.

"Grandfather Sidney regularly supplied the liners leaving Southampton Docks with fresh produce. On the occasion when the *Titanic* left on her maiden voyage, Sidney was on the dockside, having delivered a cartload of vegetables. An old seafarer said to him,

"Aye, she's a lovely ship, but I'm sorry to say she won't be coming back. See for yourself, there's not a single seagull following her out!"

Later, Grandfather took over the tenancy of Bargain Farm. Their son, Ralph, still farms there:

In 1948 we learned that our land was to be compulsorily purchased for road widening and improvements. Dad decided that we would leave before we were forced to go, and after much searching and several disappointments, Croft Cottage Farm at Denhams Corner in Botley was chosen. After our comparative luxuries of electricity and gas cooking it was a terrible hardship to revert to oil lamps and cooking on a range. Only when new comforts were installed did we begin to love our new home."

Ralph Hurst, who is Edna De la Cour's cousin, is the last remaining farmer in the Millbrook area. He lives at Bargain Farm which is situated in a lane off Brownhill Road. Strictly speaking the farmhouse is just over the boundary line into Nursling, but the land which used to belong to Bargain Farm was in Millbrook, and the Hurst family is very much a Millbrook family, so it seems entirely appropriate to include the farm in this history.

In 1986 the farmhouse was put on the 'Listed Buildings' register as a building of architectural and

Phillip Hurst with the carthorse Captain in Bargain Farm yard in the 1950s. *Photograph courtesy of Ralph Hurst.*

No. 2

Important

WANTED—POTATOES

An Appeal to the Parishioners.

THERE IS A SHORTAGE OF BREAD

THE GERMANS are trying to starve us; but if the War were to end to-morrow there would still be, for at least a year or two, a great shortage of corn.

POTATOES FORM THE NEXT BEST SUBSTITUTE

and they can be converted into flour, without interfering with the supply for your dinner or other meals.

THEREFORE GROW MORE POTATOES!

YOU CAN HELP by growing more Potatoes in your garden, and by joining with others in cultivating, planting, hoeing, and harvesting, IN YOUR SPARE TIME, an extra acre of Potatoes in your parish. There are nearly 15,000 parishes in England and Wales. If each parish grew two extra acres of Potatoes, reckoning a yield of only six tons to the acre, that would mean an extra 180,000 tons, or 3,600,000 cwts., of Potatoes for use next season. IT WILL PAY YOU to grow them.

OUR FIGHTING MEN ARE LOOKING TO YOU TO BACK THEM UP. DON'T YOU LET THEM DOWN!

The Rural League, 21, Surrey Street, Strand, W.C.

"I was brought up in farming all my life, there was nothing else I could do. I went to Millbrook School up at Green Lane. Mr. Weston used to take us for gardening lessons. I thought he was a very nice man. There weren't any animals, it was just like an allotment. He didn't teach us anything scientific, it was just the basics of gardening like double digging, the old fashioned ways. I enjoyed it, I was always interested in gardening. I always had to help with the work when I got home from school. Over the road there, where they've built Danebury Way, Mum had a big lot of chickens and as soon as I got home I had to feed and water them and collect the eggs. The chickens were all free range.

"When my father took over the farm it was about 120 acres, then after I left school and came to work on the farm, he took some more land on Mansel Road. In the end he was farming over 300 acres. The land went right from Redbridge Lane over to Green Lane. He also had ground at Lower Wimpson Farm and over in Redbridge where the gas holder is. Lower Wimpson Farm had a huge brick-walled yard with barns, pig sties, a granary and a dairy. He grew corn and a lot of vegetables, we used to have eight men working full-time on the farm and fourteen women working part-time. Most of them were working on the land, and we had a couple of men helping in the dairy. We used to have a herd of 40 or 50 cows in the fields round the farmhouse and the rest of the cattle were down at Wimpson Farm. The cattle were all out on the grazing and they had to be brought in to milk twice a day. The dairy was over in the yard here at Bargain Farm.

"When I left school I had to look after 300 pigs, feed them and muck them out. They were all in pig sties or sheds, not in the open fields. I used to go down to Nursling station and fetch lorry loads of potatoes to feed the pigs. After the war the Government used to buy up surplus crops and sell them on very cheaply for animal feed. They'd be sent in railway wagons and you had to go and shovel them out yourself, 22 tons at a time.

"During the war we used to grow a lot of vegetables for the armed forces, the vegetables were sent to the army camps. Sometimes Dad would stay out ploughing the land all night with the old tractor, he had so much to do. Tractors were only just 'coming in' during the war and when I left school to work on the farm we still used mostly cart horses. Before the war all the ploughing was done with horses, my Dad and Grandfather before him did it that way, but I never did horse ploughing. By the time I was old enough to do the job the tractor was in service.

"I worked for Dad on the farm from when I left school in 1951 at fifteen, until I had to go in the army for National Service at eighteen. I went abroad in 1954, and when I came back all this land from Brownhill Road towards Southampton had been taken and was built on. There was vast development there all at once, it all happened between 1954 and 1956. I was very surprised when I came back, I hardly recognised the place. It was compulsorily purchased. Dad was left with this piece of land in the triangle where the farmhouse is and a small piece down at Foxes Farm and some over near the railway line. From over 300 acres we'd gone down to just about 100 acres. As the farm dwindled we had to get rid of the labourers. We still grew the vegetables, we sold them down in the Southampton wholesale market in Bernard Street. It was my job to take the stuff down there when I came out of the army and I could drive the van.

"We always had good relations with the other farmers round here, there were the Govers at Upper Wimpson Farm, Pearces had Yew Tree Farm, and there were the Tuffins. There were four farms in Mansel Road. Upper Wimpson farmhouse was a beautiful place, really old-fashioned. Bargain Farm goes back to the fourteenth or fifteenth century. All the farmers round here were from old local families, they were all cousins or distantly related in some way. They were mostly mixed farms, Joe Gover did a lot of vegetables, but Bob Gover had all cattle. You never used to see a lot of sheep round here.

"Of course they were all turned out when the land was compulsorily purchased. Joe Gover went to land up by the Romsey Golf Course, his grandson's still

Lower Wimpson Farm which stood in the area now enclosed by Evenlode Road, Derwent Road and Mansel Road East. *Southampton City Archives.*

there now. Bob Gover died shortly afterwards, but I'm not sure about the others. My Dad took some more land at Nursling Street, but that's been built on now as well. I've managed to rub along all these years. I've got a couple of pigs, two sows and twelve babies. I'm more or less retired now but my two sons are carrying on, they live locally. We still grow vegetables and sell what we can in the farm shop. We take some into the market in Southampton and we supply some local shops. The price we get for our stuff is ridiculous, terrible. The state of farming today is so uncertain, you just don't know what is going to happen. The trouble with having such a limited amount of land is that you start to get problems with pests and diseases, you can't keep to the proper crop rotation, club root is a real nuisance in the cabbages. We mostly grow potatoes, cabbages, cauliflowers, and leeks. I started doing bedding plants in the greenhouse in about 1985, there's a good outlet for those, we ought to build that side up. It's all very different to what it was in the past. There's only my two sons and me working on the farm now, and a lad who helps part-time at the weekend. We don't get any women coming in for picking the vegetables, they won't do it these days, too dirty.

"I don't think we'll have this land much longer. In my five-acre field they're building a roundabout to take all the traffic from the new hotel and the new houses that are going behind it. I said to my nippers,

"I bet you, when they've got that roundabout in, they'll put another road across my fields at the back and build on this land. I reckon all I'll be left with is the house."

BIBLIOGRAPHY

Gallaher, T.: *Southampton Inns and Taverns.*

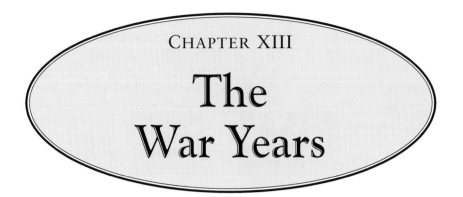

CHAPTER XIII

The War Years

Perhaps the most dramatic years in Millbrook's long history were those of the Second World War when the village was not only a front-line target for enemy attacks, but played such an important part in the struggle for victory.

As the situation in Europe deteriorated, local authorities started to prepare for emergencies. The Air Raid Precautions Committee was set up to arrange the provision of gas masks, public shelters and sirens. Training was given in first aid, ambulance drivers were recruited, lists were made of available vehicles, decontamination stations were set up and sandbags filled. In February 1939 a trench shelter for 424 persons was built on Millbrook Recreation Ground and another public shelter was planned outside Toogoods, opposite Millbrook railway station. In May 1939 the Home Office suggested that the pace of preparations should be accelerated. A.R.P. (Air Raid Precautions) posts were set up at Foundry Lane school, in Millbrook Recreation Ground, in the old school building at

Wimpson, in King George's Avenue, at Mill Mead in Oakley Road, and at Cracknore Road.

One controversial aspect of the preparations for war was that the Home Office decided that Millbrook was to be considered a 'safe' area and that schoolchildren did not need to be evacuated. In fact plans were made for evacuees from other areas to be billeted in Millbrook and to attend the school. There was outrage when villagers received Government pamphlets about the billeting scheme. The clerk of Millbrook Parish Council, C. J. Godden, wrote to Romsey and Stockbridge Rural District Council (Millbrook and other rural parishes formed an amalgamated District Council under this title) on 20 January 1939 protesting vigorously:

"The outcry which has taken place on the receipt by householders of the pamphlet issued to them on the matter, guides the Council as to the general feeling, that instead of taking evacuated persons, a scheme

Dragon's Teeth anti-tank defences in Millbrook Road, February 1945. These were situated between Boundary Close and King George's Avenue. The gap between the houses shows the position of Tanners Brook. The old Royal Mail public house can be seen in the distance on the right. *Southampton City Archives.*

should be prepared for the evacuation of children from Millbrook. It is understood that Southampton is No. 2 danger zone outside London, and in view of the fact that the Docks abuts the borders of the parish, and the parish has within it a large Railway Depot and communicating bridge, that Millbrook would be in the very midst of danger from air attack, and therefore the Council are of the opinion that reception of evacuated persons should not be considered for this parish."

The Ministry remained unmoved and plans for the reception of 442 children had to be made. In protest, the Parish Council refused to appoint a billeting officer, and in May 1939 the Ministry agreed to a slight concession, that if there was sufficient accommodation available in other areas it might not be necessary to use Millbrook. Then on 17 June 1939 Gerald Palmer M.P. wrote to the Parish Council saying that 5,600 persons had been allocated to Millbrook, half of them school-children, and that Millbrook must be used for this purpose. In the event, nothing like this number of evacuees actually arrived. However, some children did come from Portsmouth, Gosport and London. I was lucky enough to be able to find one of them, still living in Millbrook.

Dennis Hale used to have the nick-name of 'Ginger', he described his experiences as a wartime evacuee at Millbrook School. He was evacuated in September 1939 and for part of the time he lived in Nursling before moving into Redbridge Lane in Millbrook.

"I lived in Portsmouth and we were evacuated. I was only ten when I went, with my little gas mask round my neck. I wasn't too worried about going because I never had much home-life anyway. I was brought up by my Dad, and he had a corner shop so he was always busy.

"I can remember standing outside the picture house in our road waiting for the bus to come and then getting on a train, but I can't remember anything about packing or getting ready to go. We got on another bus out to Nursling, to the school, and we were distributed all over the place. Honestly I can't remember what happened, it was all so strange, things were going on all around me, different kiddies, different people milling around. Everything happened so fast. My brothers were older than me and they weren't evacuated, so I was all on my own. I finished up with six other boys living with Mr. Bull, one of our teachers, and his wife, in the bungalow behind Grove Place at Nursling. I was with six complete strangers, I didn't know any of the other boys, or Mr and Mrs Bull, and none of my friends from school was anywhere near.

"In Grove Place at the beginning of the War they had a chauffeur and a butler and about six maids, a cook and a housekeeper and four or five gardeners, and all the rest of it! Our meals were sent over from the big house, I don't ever remember Mrs. Bull doing any cooking for us. We slept three to a room, but I thought it was very comfortable. I'd come from living in a house where the front room was turned into shop and the back room was full of stores so it was very cramped. We were allowed to play in the gardens and they gave us our own apple tree so that we could pick the fruit, it was September you see. It was a beautiful place with kitchen gardens and everything. We were amazed, coming from Portsmouth we hardly ever saw a tree. It was all so new to us, we were in wonderment.

"The family at the big house was called the Magniacs. At Christmas they sent over a nice book for me, *Black Beauty*. We weren't invited over to the house for a Christmas party or anything, the family never mixed with us at all. They never even came over to see us. Sometimes we'd see the lady of the house in the distance, but that was all the contact we had with them.

"The gardeners were smashing to us, and the maids were good as well, they'd come to the window and talk to us and make a fuss of us. Of course I liked that, never having had a mother. They did our washing as well, we never had to do any chores for ourselves. We didn't have many toys so we'd just read or play games amongst ourselves in the evenings.

"I was happy there, but it didn't last. After a few months Mr and Mrs Bull went back to Portsmouth, and then the gardeners were all called up and the maids left to do war work. There was nobody to look after the big house, let alone us children, so we had to move.

"We were sent to a big house opposite Nursling Church. I was a very unhappy kid there, I didn't like the place at all, it was such a dismal house. For some reason I hated the housekeeper, I didn't understand what I'd done wrong but we just couldn't get along.

"I only stayed there four weeks and then I was moved again and I was sent by myself to live with Mrs Hawkins in Redbridge Lane. I stayed there until I left school when I was fourteen. Mrs Hawkins didn't have electricity or gas, we had oil lamps. I can remember having the old tin bath out in the kitchen to get bathed once a week, Mrs Hawkins heated up the water in a boiler out in the scullery. She used a little Primus stove and the open fire to do the cooking. I don't know how she managed, but we had cracking meals. We always lived well because they used to grow as many vegetables as they could, and Mr Hawkins worked on the railways and sometimes the train would knock over pheasants and rabbits and he could stop and pick them up. Meat was ever so scarce during the war, so it was a rare treat if we had rabbit stew or roast pheasant. Mrs Hawkins' dad worked out at Mottisfont as a Head Gardener, so we had lots of lovely fruit. We used to listen to the radio a lot, the news and so on. When I was living there, the radio was powered by an accumulator, a thing like a battery, which used to be charged up at the local garage. So if we wanted to listen to the radio I was sent to collect it. I really enjoyed living there, she was very good to me. Dad often came to see me. My brother came too after he'd been rescued from Dunkirk, that must have been in 1940, but dates don't mean much to you when you're a kid.

"At first I went to the school in Nursling Street, but as soon as I was eleven I was transferred to Millbrook School in Green Lane. My dad bought me a bicycle so I could get to school, he was quite well off as he had the shop. By that time us evacuees were more or less integrated with the other kids, I don't suppose half of them knew I was evacuated. I was just accepted as one of the boys. I was never a great scholar. Reading, writing, geography, history, I was all right with all of those, but I couldn't do arithmetic to save my life. I was always in trouble, I was always stood outside the door. I used to talk and do silly things.

"The headmaster was Mr. Mackay; we called him 'Tec'. He was just like a detective, he'd sneak around the corridors and he'd be sure to sniff you out if you were doing anything wrong. Many's the time I had the cane from that man. I suppose I used to fight and get into trouble and give the teachers a bit of back-chat, but if I was stood outside the classroom door you could be sure 'Tec' would come along. He'd say:

'Up to my room! What were you doing?'

'I was talking, sir.'

'Right, two of the best for you.'

So it was – Whack! Whack! – and that was it, back to the classroom. Of course being ginger I always stood out, and people noticed if I was doing something wrong.

"The Woodwork teacher was another man I didn't like, he'd hit you round the head with a bit of wood if he thought you were misbehaving. He was one of our Portsmouth teachers who was evacuated with us. He bullied you into doing things, he didn't stand and explain things. We used to go gardening. The plots were alongside Green Lane, we grew a lot of vegetables. I used to enjoy that for the afternoon.

"There were six air-raid shelters in the playing field up near Romsey Road. When the sirens went we had to come out of the classrooms and run across the field to the shelters, it was quite a long way. The shelters were half sunk in the ground and half above it and had benches all along the sides. When we were in the shelters we used to sing, there was one particular nipper called Grace who always sang and we joined in. We sang all the war-time favourites. The teachers didn't try to go on with lessons or anything, it was too dark, we only had candles. Sometimes we would be in there for ages, but we weren't afraid, when you're a kid things just wash over you, it was more like an adventure. When we came out we'd be laughing and joking, we didn't realise how serious it all was. There were quite a few raids. One boy from Portsmouth and his sister were killed, they'd been evacuated to a house in Rownhams which was hit by a land mine. I don't remember being particularly upset. I remember people talking about it, but I didn't seem to take it in, there were so many things happening to me."

The Parish Magazine for October 1939 contained an encouraging message from the Rector, Revd. J. L. Beaumont James:

"War, alas, has come! I came to Millbrook in the dark days of 1917 during the last war, another gigantic contest is upon us. What we have to face is a new form of warfare, never hitherto experienced in

Bomb damage at the White House Garage. *Photographed by E. Phillips and reproduced by kind permission of Jennifer Robinson.*

James Brindley Nicolson V.C., D.F.C.

England, in which whole fleets of aeroplanes may come over. The population who have to stay because of their work can be relied upon to show truly English fortitude and good humour."

The feared air-raids did not come during the first months of the war, a period known as the 'Phoney War', but the Rector warned:

"Some will think that we were foolish to try to get Millbrook children evacuated when no raids have occurred but the danger is not yet over."

The Rector was proved right. The first bombs to fall on Southampton actually fell on Millbrook. A German bomber, presumably trying to destroy the King George V Graving Dock, dropped a stick of bombs which left a trail of destruction.

Air-raid report. 11.19 p.m. 19th June 1940

I beg to report that on Wednesday June 19th an air-raid warning was received at 23.19 hours. Reconnaissance showed that two high explosive bombs had fallen in South Mill Road, one in Westbury Road, one at the entrance to the Tobacco Factory and three in Millbrook Road. Six casualties in the raid, two of a serious nature. A large fire broke out in Millbrook Road where the White House Garage suffered a direct hit on the petrol pump station.

After the British forces had been driven out of France at Dunkirk in June 1940, Hitler laid plans for the invasion of England the following September. First he had to get control in the air, and the summer of 1940 saw the Battle of Britain commence as the German Luftwaffe attempted to smash the Royal Air Force out of the skies over Britain. On 13 August 1940 the Luftwaffe launched a massive offensive intended to destroy aircraft and air-fields.

These were frightening times and the Rector wrote in the Parish Magazine:

"The war enters its most critical phase. On the Continent the campaign is completed and lost. On the shores of England it has to be fought and won. We fight on alone, abandoned by Man, we put our whole trust in God. Already Millbrook feels the horror of war."

Many people living in southern England watched as dog fights between German aircraft and British Spitfires and Hurricanes took place above them. No incident could have been more dramatic than one which took place over Millbrook on 16 August 1940. There are numerous different accounts of the events which took place, and it is difficult to know the truth about some details.

Flight Lieutenant James Brindley Nicolson was despatched from Boscombe Down with 249 Squadron to patrol between Poole and Romsey. Nicolson led Red Section in Hurricane P3576 and was accompanied by Squadron Leader Eric King and Pilot Officer Martyn King. For his bravery on that day, Nicolson was awarded the Victoria Cross, the only one to be awarded to Fighter Command during World War II. James Nicolson described the action shortly after his award had been announced. The account is abridged and comes from an unidentified newspaper cutting:

"The sun was shining from a cloudless sky and there was hardly a breath of wind. Our squadron was going towards Southampton on patrol at 15,000 feet when I saw three Junkers 88 bombers about four miles away. We chased hard after them, but when we were about a mile behind we saw the 88s fly straight into a squadron of Spitfires and I guessed it was curtains for the Junkers. I was right and they were all shot down in quick time. So we swung round again and started to climb up to 18,000 feet over Southampton, to rejoin our squadron. I was still a long way from the squadron when suddenly, very close in rapid succession, I heard four big bangs. They were the loudest noises I had ever heard and they had been made by four cannon shells from a Messerschmitt 110 hitting my machine."

Nicolson was badly injured by these shots, his face and foot received shrapnel wounds and a fire was started in the cockpit which caused severe burns to his hands and body. In the heat of battle he was unaware of the extent of his injuries. The story continues:

"I started cursing myself for my carelessness. I was

just thinking of jumping out when suddenly a Messerschmitt 110 whizzed under me and got right in my gunsights. I pressed the gun button, for the Messerschmitt was in nice range, I plugged him the first time and I could see my tracer bullets entering the German machine. He was going like mad, twisting and turning as he tried to get away from my fire. Both of us must have been doing about 400 mph as we went down together in a dive. I shouted out loud to him: 'I'll teach you some manners!' I knew I was getting him nearly all the time I was firing. By this time it was pretty hot inside my machine from the burst petrol tank. Well I gave the German all I had, and the last I saw of him was when he was going down, with his right wing lower than the left wing. I decided it was about time I left the aircraft and baled out. I began to float down, then an aircraft, a Messerschmitt I think, came tearing past me. I decided to pretend I was dead, and hung limply by the parachute straps. The Messerschmitt came back once, but I didn't get the bullets I was half expecting. When I got lower I saw I was in danger of coming down in the sea, so I wriggled about a bit and managed to float inland and aimed at a nice open field. I had a piece of good news almost immediately. One of the people who came along and who had watched the combat, said they had seen the Messerschmitt 110 dive straight into the sea."

The two other planes in Nicolson's Red Section were also hit. Squadron Leader King was able to get his Hurricane back to Boscombe Down, but Pilot Officer King had to bale out of his aircraft and he was killed when his parachute collapsed. He fell into the garden of 30, Clifton Road, Shirley. The other Messerschmitt involved in this incident left the area. According to Observer Corps log books of that date, the Hurricanes came down, one in the vicinity of Hoe Farm to the north of Rownhams and south-east of Romsey, and the other on fields to the west of Nursling Church. The evidence is unclear and other witnesses have suggested that one site was on the corner of Baker's Drove and Rownhams Lane and the other was at Lee, near Romsey.

In his own account of the events, Nicolson omitted to mention that he had been fired on as he was coming down to land. It is certain that he was hit by 'friendly fire' but there was considerable controversy about who actually fired the shots. At the time it was claimed that the Local Defence Volunteers (the Home Guard) had mistaken him for a German pilot and had shot at him as he descended. However, Mr R. W. F. Stanley, who was first on the scene, and was himself an LDV, strongly refuted this and said that it was in fact regular soldiers from The Royal Engineers stationed near Sparshatt's garage and some Canadian troops based in the Docks. Some 0.303 cartridge cases were found near the scene, and these were a type not used by the LDVs. Nicolson himself did not wish the matter to be pursued, as at the time things were bad enough without putting anyone on the mat for the shooting, it would degrade the regular troops. (This information was obtained from an account written by Mr. Stanley in 1986.)

After recovering from his injuries, Nicolson returned to flying in April 1941 as a Squadron Leader. He died whilst flying on a mission over the Bay of Bengal on 2 May 1945.

On the thirtieth anniversary of the event in 1970 a plaque was unveiled on a spot near where he landed, this is now within the Philips Semiconductors Plant in Millbrook Road. It was re-dedicated in August 1990 on the fiftieth anniversary.

> **On or near this spot on the 16th August 1940, during the Battle of Britain, the late Wing Commander (then Flight Lieutenant) J. B. Nicolson V.C. D.F.C. R.A.F. of No. 249 Squadron, landed after parachuting from his burning Hurricane following an engagement with the enemy. After being hit and his aircraft set on fire, he continued with the action and was successful in destroying an Me110 before abandoning his aircraft. For this act of gallantry he was awarded the Victoria Cross, the only pilot of Fighter Command to be so honoured during World War II.**

This incident was both heroic and tragic, but seen through the eyes of a child it was just very exciting. Whilst adults were anxious and fearful, children took the drama of the war in their stride and even enjoyed it.

Al Donovan, who after a career in 'show biz', still lives in Millbrook, witnessed the incident. His account evokes the feeling of boyish adventure, which many children must have felt during the war:

"My friend Jack was my mentor, he was four years older than me, so I looked up to him in everything I did. He was thirteen and I was nine. We spent all our time playing at 'The Swamp', which was a boggy, tree-filled area near Warren Avenue, it's now been made into a proper playing field. We climbed trees and swung from ropes and even made a pulley glide from some discarded barrage balloon wire that we found. There was hardly any school at that time because if you had a disturbed night with air raids you didn't have to go in to lessons the next day. So as far as we were concerned, every night was a disturbed night.

"On this particular August day we were playing in 'The Swamp' when the sirens sounded. We didn't take any notice, we were used to sirens, but after a while the gunfire became quite intense and Jack decided we ought to go home. We both lived in Winchester Road, and as we ran along Warren

Avenue, some grown-ups told us to get down and take cover, so we went into a public air-raid shelter in Jones's building yard. When the ack-ack gunfire eased off we decided to make our way home. When we reached the junction of Winchester Road and Warren Avenue, where the ground is quite high, we heard aircraft engines and we could see two Hurricanes and a Messerschmitt over Millbrook. The British planes were on fire. As we watched, a pilot tumbled from each of them. As they fell, their chutes opened, we'd never seen parachutes before. We watched them descend and what happened to their planes became secondary in importance, they just flew on in flames. The Messerschmitt was going on across Millbrook, but then it turned and came back. We were transfixed watching this. One pilot was hanging motionless under his parachute as if he was dead. Then we heard gunfire from the enemy plane and the other pilot's parachute collapsed, the canopy made what they call a Roman Candle, it went into a thin, useless, wavering column. We watched this dreadful event with the pilot struggling in his harness, his legs and arms kicking, he just fell. It was terrible to see him, and it has etched itself on my memory to this day. This took our attention away from the first man (who we later discovered was Flight Lieutenant Nicolson), but after the other pilot had disappeared from view, presumably having crashed to earth, we watched him drifting over Millbrook and coming down in the fields.

"Now Jack's Uncle Stan was an ARP Warden, so he got to know about things, and he told us that Pilot Officer Martyn King had fallen into a garden in the Clifton Road area and had indeed been killed.

"Air-raids were a frequent occurrence at this time and Jack and I established a habit that when the all-clear sounded after night-time raids, we would go to our front doors and wave to each other to say we were all right before turning in to go to bed. The night after the aeroplane incident there was yet another raid, and it was not until about half past four in the morning that Jack and I were able to make our customary wave to each other. On this occasion he came across the road and told me that Uncle Stan knew where one of the Hurricanes had crashed, out at Nursling near the Horns Inn. Jack said he was going to borrow his uncle's bike and cycle out there to get a souvenir, and I could come too, but I just wanted to go to bed.

"Later on that morning Jack invited me round to see his prize, and I was dumbfounded. I was expecting some small piece of wreckage that you could handle, but he had a whole section of the tail, it was wonderful. He had cycled out to Nursling and found the plane in a field. There were no Home Guard men keeping an eye on it, so he climbed the fence and went to see what he could find. He picked up this large piece of the tail and was amazed at how light it was. He then proceeded to put it on the saddle of his bike and wheeled it all the way home. At the bottom of Romsey Road, by 'The Old Thatched House' he came across a group of soldiers and he was a bit worried what they would do, but they just watched him go past and never said a word.

"You may wonder what happened to this section of the Hurricane. Uncle Stan and Jack took it to bits and made use of some pieces from it, but then they began to get worried that they might get into trouble for taking it. So Jack and Uncle Stan dug a huge hole behind the air-raid shelter in the garden and simply buried it. After the War the row of cottages, St. James' Row, was demolished, and eventually a garage was built on the site, between Grange Road and Medina Road. When they dug the foundations they must have come across Jack's souvenir, but nothing ever appeared in the papers about the mysterious wreckage!"

Throughout August, British fighter pilots challenged the German Luftwaffe, but by 15 September 1940 it had become clear to Hitler that there would be no Nazi domination of the skies over Britain and the planned invasion was postponed. Instead Hitler switched targets from airfields to cities and the Blitz began. According to the diaries of Mrs. Goulty who lived in Shirley and kept a record of every raid throughout the war, there were 359 raids in 1940, culminating in the terrible attacks on the nights of 23 and 30 November, and 1 December, when the city centre was destroyed. In 1941 there were 509 alerts, and thereafter the number decreased, with 227 alerts in 1943. In June 1944 flying bombs were a new hazard. The last air-raid alert was from 7.40 to 7.50 p.m. on Sunday 5 November 1944. It is difficult to imagine how terrifying it must have been to live through this period.

Jean Barker, who is still a Millbrook resident, was a girl at the time and vividly describes the experience of being bombed out:

Air raid damage to Millbrook goods yard. *Photograph courtesy of Associated British Ports, Port of Southampton.*

"I went to Foundry Lane School and when the war started we were evacuated to Christchurch, I was eleven, my sister was thirteen and my brother was nine. I remember we set off from the Terminus station with our gas masks and our names on labels on our coats. We were so unhappy and homesick. My sister and I were in the same house and they seemed to think we were there to do all the housework. We had to wash up and clean windows and dig the garden and plant the potatoes. We even had to creosote the fence that went right round the garden, they seemed to forget we were only children. Four of us from school decided to run away and walk back to Southampton, but we were picked up and taken to the police station, so we had to go back. My brother eventually became ill he was so homesick, so after we had been evacuated nearly a year our older sister was sent to fetch us home.

"We actually came home just in time for the worst bombing. If it was a clear night my Dad would say, 'It's a bomber's moon,' because the moonlight would show up Southampton Water so clearly, all the bombers had to do was follow the river and they knew the docks were at the end of it.

"One night there was an air raid on and we were all sitting in the Anderson shelter in our back garden, it was freezing cold. A bomb scored a direct hit on top of us. The force of the bomb hitting the top of the air-raid shelter was incredible, the compression made you feel as if you were melting, as if a ton weight had fallen on your head. It didn't explode, it bounced off the top of the shelter into the soft soil, it must have been a delayed action time bomb. We climbed out and then the air-raid warden came running up shouting that we had to get out, the bomb could go off at any minute. We grabbed up some blankets that we'd taken into the shelter and piled them into an old doll's pram and ran off up Freshfield Road towards the Tobacco factory where they had a public shelter. The raid was still going on, it was terrifying, you could hear the planes overhead and loud explosions, and the ack-ack guns were going, firing at the bombers when the searchlights picked them out. We had to get round a crater where a bomb had fallen in Freshfield Road, all in the dark of the blackout of course. Mother stopped to be sick over someone's fence, I suppose it was nerves. I waited for her while Father went on ahead with my little brother. The public shelter was very narrow and had benches each side to sit on, but it was so cramped that the grown-ups knees touched in the middle. Down one end there was a sort of curtain made of sacking and a bucket behind it, that was the toilet.

"When we came out in the morning we had nowhere to live. The bomb that had fallen in our garden hadn't exploded, but we couldn't go back to the house in case it did. We didn't know what to do, so we just sat on the edge of the pavement in Waterhouse Lane. I remember there was a thick hoar frost and every blade of grass was white, my teeth wouldn't stop chattering, I was so cold. Suddenly a WVS van appeared at the end of the road and they gave us all a mug of tea and a corned beef sandwich, I think that's the best meal I ever had in my life. We were just like refugees because all we had were the clothes we were wearing and a doll's pram full of blankets. First we went to a reception centre up in Park Road where they served meals for people who had been bombed out, but then we went to my grandmother's house over at Lodge Road in Portswood. The bomb disposal team eventually got round to our bomb but they couldn't dig it out of the waterlogged soil and in the end they had to detonate it, so our house was more or less destroyed. I remember going back and seeing a row of cup handles hanging up in the remains of the kitchen, only the handles, the cups had gone.

"Mother went down to the Civic Centre about finding somewhere to live permanently and they let us have a house on Millbrook Road. There was a whole row of houses empty near The Sailor's Return pub, apparently nobody would live in them because they were so near the docks and people felt like sitting ducks in them. Later on in the war, from our front windows we could see them building the Mulberry harbours for the D-Day landings in the King George V Graving Dock."

Millbrook Church was damaged in several raids in 1940 and the rectory was requisitioned for military use. The Rector went to live at Blighmont House until January 1942 and announced that in cases of emergency he was prepared to marry members of H.M. forces or mercantile marine on Sundays during the war. After the severe raids of November 1940 he wrote:

"The courage of the populace in danger and the fortitude of those in suffering is magnificent. Even as I write these words the sirens are sounding and the buzz of planes grows louder."

Edna De la Cour lived just near Millbrook Pond during the war years and she too has described her experience of air-raids:

"The war got progressively worse and soon we were to know the horror of air raids, which started long before we had been issued with an Anderson shelter. The sirens would wail to warn us of imminent danger, whereupon we would be hauled from our warm beds, hustled downstairs into the living room, and there we huddled together on the floor with our backs to the centre wall. The large wooden shutters, which we were thankful to have, were closed across the window and somehow Dad managed to prop the kitchen table against them as well. Everyone became jittery, Dad in particular was very nervous and apprehensive of the nightly danger. By this time, his means of transport had progressed to a small green van. In an effort to get as far away as possible from the town and docks where bombing was targeted, Dad decided to load the whole family into his new vehicle and drive to Baddesley to spend night time in the woods. Mum sat in the front with baby Alan in her arms, Mary and I in the back accompanied by our lodger, Mrs Arney, and Mum's younger brother, Ron, who also lived with us. In cold and very cramped conditions I shall never know how any of us managed to sleep. At daybreak we would return home, always wondering if our house would still be standing.

"After a time, a new public air-raid shelter came into use. It was built above ground on the corner opposite The Swan public house, and for a while we used this facility. It became very crowded and uncomfortable on cold concrete seats, and we were pleased when Dad, with the help of Ron and neighbours, had installed our own haven of safety, the Anderson air-raid shelter. Arched panels of corrugated steel were bolted together to form a short tunnel. Although it was only about ten feet long, Dad constructed timber bunk beds to accommodate all the family. There was just enough room for a seat on either side of the doorway for Mrs Arney, the lodger, and Mrs Robinson, who lived in the caravan in Dad's field.

"As raids became more frequent it soon became a regular ritual, night after night, to have to leave the comfort of our beds, pulling on warm garments which were left at the ready. I would never leave the house without my dolls, and with them clutched in my arms, I remember stumbling out into the pitch darkness of the blackout, across the yard and along a narrow path skirting the strawshed and hayrick, to reach the steps leading down into the shelter. Poor Mrs Arney was so nervous and anxious to get underground that she would give Mary and me a hefty push and send us flying down the flight of six steps. This upheaval soon became too much to bear, so for a time we took to settling in the shelter from mid-evening onwards.

"When the raids became intense it was impossible to sleep. We would listen with bated breath as aircraft droned overhead, trying to distinguish the nearby guns- either the deep thump of the Nursling unit, or the sharp crack of the ack-ack gun over in old Southwell's field. But the most terrifying noise was the whistle of bombs followed by a resounding thud, its intensity depending on the closeness of the target. We could also hear the fragments of shells landing on the pigsty roofs. In the early morning light when we emerged from our hole in the ground we never knew whether the house would still be intact or merely a pile of rubble. Luckily the worst that happened was smashed windows when a land-mine fell in the orchard behind the Post Office, just about where Homebase stands today.

"After a particularly heavy night raid on Southampton, it was a pitiful sight indeed to see a steady stream of homeless people trundling along the road outside our house. Some were very old, many had babies in prams, or pushed little hand carts. They had lost everything overnight and walked along not knowing where they were going, but aiming for the sanctuary of the Forest. In the early morning mist they looked like ghosts emerging from hell."

During this period of bombing raids the work of the Air Raid Precautions (ARP) units was vital. The wardens had many duties; they had to check that every house was properly blacked out and not showing any chinks of light which might guide enemy aircraft, they had to check gas masks, supervise public shelters, and in the event of raids they helped to co-ordinate the work of the emergency services.

One of these ARP wardens was **Joyce Hillier**, she was based at the post in Foundry Lane School. Years later, she went on to become the Foundry Lane secretary and researched the history of the school after her retirement. Sadly, Joyce died just a few weeks after telling me about her wartime experiences.

"When the War started I was sixteen. My father was away in the army, he'd volunteered although he was really too old to be called up straightaway. He was one of the 'Old Contemptibles' from the First World War. (They were soldiers who volunteered early in the War and were part of the British Expeditionary Force which went to France to fight. The German Kaiser called them 'A contemptible little army'.) My mother wasn't very pleased about him volunteering, I can remember her voice going on and on about it: 'Why did you have to go and volunteer, didn't you do enough in the last lot?'

"We all had to do something to help so I became an ARP Warden. The first ARP Post that I was in was at the old Chest Hospital. That's the Western Community Hospital and Tescos now. The man in charge of the Post was a friend of my boss, so he knew me and knew I was trained, and he said: 'We want someone on the switchboard who won't get in a 'funk', you'd better come.'

"I was there for a while and then my mother said she wanted me to come to the ARP Post at Regents Park School where she was working as a telephonist. I was only sixteen and we did as we were told in those days, so I went. After a time I was transferred to the Post in Foundry Lane School and I stayed there until the end of the War. That ARP building was there until a couple of years ago as the caretaker's hut, it was pulled down when they made alterations.

After I finished work I would come home for my tea and then, if I was on duty, I would go down to the ARP Post. One of the duties was to go round the streets checking that everyone kept the 'blackout' properly. You had to have thick curtains which didn't let the light through. They had to be drawn tight so that not a chink of light was showing which might guide the bombers. If people had been careless and you could see any lamps shining, you had to bang on the door and tell them to put the lights out. Another duty was checking the gas masks. Every so often the Wardens would call on all the households and ask to see the gas masks and test them with a special kit.

"We would get a 'phone call telling us if an air raid was coming our way, it was a 'Red Alert' if the bombers looked as if they were targeting our area. The information came from the RAF, they plotted the course of the enemy planes and they could see where they were heading. Then the Fire Alarm bell would go off. In the early part of the War the firemen had a little fire appliance which was attached to the back of a private car. A Warden who had a car would come on duty at the ARP Post and if there was a fire he would hitch the trailer on the back of his car and drive off to deal with it.

"When the air raid warning came, some of the Wardens would be sent out on patrol, because if you were out on the street you could spot trouble, which you couldn't if you were down in the shelter. There was nothing to say you couldn't go down to the shelter, but generally you stayed on duty. Someone, often a Boy Scout, would run round the public shelters and make sure there was a proper Warden in charge in them, and take messages, that sort of thing.

"I can remember a funny incident that happened to one lady on patrol duty. One night there was an 'Alert' on and Mrs Cross, one of the senior Wardens, was running round the streets blowing her whistle to warn people to go to their shelters. She blew so hard that she blew her false teeth out. Well, you can imagine what it was like trying to find a set of teeth on the road in the pitch dark of the blackout. She was gone for such a long time that we thought she must have had an accident, so we went to search for her. Eventually we found her, still looking for her teeth, so we all joined in, crawling around in the street until someone discovered them

"We had quite a few casualties in this area during the Blitz in 1940 and a classroom in the Foundry Lane Infants' School was made into a temporary mortuary. We had several very bad raids in November and December 1940. One night I'd come home from work and after tea I washed my hair. I was just putting it in curlers when the air raid sirens started up. Mum said: 'We'd better get down to the ARP Post, I think we're in for it tonight.'

"But we were too late, we didn't even have time to get to our own shelter in the garden. The raid had started and I never did finish doing my hair. Suddenly it seemed as though the house went up in the air and came down again and all the windows and doors blew out. I dived under the dining room table, it was a big, old-fashioned one, and my mother dived under it from the other side, and we just lay there waiting for things to calm down. I said to Mum: 'Mum, if I'd been killed, would they have buried me in my curlers?' I wasn't worried about being killed, but I didn't want to be buried in my curlers. It just shows you the stupid things you worry about in these situations.

"The houses next to us had a direct hit and were completely flattened and the people were killed. We had to leave our house as the roof was gone and the next day I came back to try to pick up some of my belongings. As I walked down the road I could see a stretcher outside our house with some bundles on it. I guessed what was in them. I had just gone in to our house when a Warden knocked on the door. He said: 'Can we come and have a look in your garden? We've found an arm and a hand on the roof and we think that there might be some more bits further down the garden.' Well of course you automatically go out with them, and we had got so far down the garden path when he stopped and said that I'd better go back indoors. I said: 'Don't worry, I'm ARP, I'm not likely to faint on you.'

"It was a head that they had found. Those houses have all been demolished and new ones built now. They came and put a tarpaulin over our roof after a few days and then we were able to move back in and live in the downstairs rooms, but we were the only people around here for a while. For a long time there were bits of clothing flapping about up in the tops of trees. You can still see some shrapnel holes in our garden wall. My friend and her Aunt were killed when their shelter got a direct hit over in Imperial Avenue.

"Once the Southampton Blitz was over in 1940 things calmed down a bit and we didn't have so many raids, though there were still daylight raids when people were killed.

"After the War was over I married my boyfriend who I'd known since we were fourteen, he was a Millbrook boy. He came back from being a Prisoner of War of the Japanese, building the Burma Railway, the Railway of Death as they called it, and the bridge over the River Kwai. He'd only just had his 21st birthday when he was captured in Singapore, but he was lucky, he came through it all and came home.

"I went back to Foundry Lane School as the secretary in 1966 and I stayed there for the next twenty years."

Many people have spoken nostalgically of the great community spirit which existed during the war, everybody wanted to 'do their bit' to help win the war. Whilst many people were conscripted, others who were too old, or too young, to serve in the Armed forces, volunteered to help defend their country. The ever popular television series, 'Dad's Army' features the efforts of the Local Defence Volunteers, later to be called the Home Guard. Initially they were very badly equipped and hardly had any proper weapons, but later they were given training, and played an invaluable role in guarding local strategic positions. e.g. In 1941, 14 Home Guard men were detailed to guard the New Docks against incendiary bombs. The volunteers were never put to the test by an invasion, but at least they were prepared to put up some resistance.

Eddie Pond, who lives in Millbrook, was one of these

The Luftwaffe photograph of the New Docks, taken on 28 August 1942. *Courtesy of Ron Williams.*

young men, and he told me about his time in the Home Guard.

"When the War broke out I was nearly fourteen and still at school. I was evacuated to Bournemouth with Regents Park School for a while, but then I turned fourteen and I had to leave school and get a job. I worked as a waiter in the White Hart pub in Shirley High Street, it isn't there any more. A lot of soldiers from the East Surrey Regiment used to come in the pub and I got quite friendly with them. They were billeted in Foundry Lane School. One night an air-raid shelter at the school got a direct hit and quite a few of them were killed. We used to go down into the cellars when a raid was on. I remember one night six houses in Waterhouse Lane, just near the pub, were blown up, and all the people in them.

"When I was just over fifteen, in 1941, my brother Don and I volunteered for 'Dad's Army'. We had some good old times, Don and I, he was seventeen. There were several other young chaps about our age and then older, more middle-aged men. We were stationed in Regents Park School, in a building that used to be Alexandra College. You had to go in the evenings after work. We didn't have any weapons at first, no guns or anything, we didn't even have a uniform for a while until we got great-coats. We used to do marching and learned how to present arms, slope arms, and so on. An old chap called Sergeant Mole was in charge. When we eventually got some guns we had shooting practice out at Romsey on a rifle range, with real bullets. I think I hit the target with one bullet out of ten! We learned to strip down and clean the guns too. Sometimes we had night manoeuvres in the fields over Oakley Road way, creeping around pretending to be Germans and British troops.

"Sometimes we had to be on guard duty outside Blighmont Barracks in the middle of the night. One time the sirens went and Don and I jumped down into the trench outside the Barracks and suddenly the sky was lit up like day. The Germans were dropping chandeliers, that's what we called flares, all over the docks. They must have been doing reconnaissance because they didn't drop any bombs that time.

"Later on I transferred to an ack-ack gun unit out at Jacob's Gutter Lane. The only time I ever got to fire the gun was on training down at Portsmouth.

"I was called up in 1944 and I was picked to be a Bevin Boy, down the coal mines. They chose you according to your call-up number."

It is interesting to note Eddie Pond's remark about the Germans "must have been doing reconnaissance" because they certainly did. Millbrook, with its New Docks and the Graving Dock was a prime target. This photograph, a copy of which was shown to me by Ron Williams, was taken by a Luftwaffe pilot in July 1942. The Graving Dock is clearly shown in the left-hand corner and the white patches reveal bombed sites. The photo was captured in Germany by American troops.

Eddie Pond spoke about being on guard duty outside the Blighmont Barracks and of course this building still stands in Millbrook Road.

Clive Milward, who works as a vehicle engineer for the Territorial Army at Blighmont Barracks, told me a little about its history. The Barracks were built in 1936 on land which was previously part of Blighmont Farm. The site was intended for use by the Territorial Army, but during World War II it was taken over by American troops. The present workshop was their cook-house and the room next to it, which was a mess room, used to have six-foot high murals of the cap badges of the American soldiers billeted there. The American troops were accommodated in wooden huts built on the site, and later, after the war, these were used by British National Servicemen.

Old maps of the area show that there was once a rifle range on Millbrook Point, but apparently this was for trainees from the St. Mary's Drill Hall in the city centre. By the time Blighmont Barracks were built, the land at Millbrook Point was involved in the reclamation scheme for the New Docks.

The building has been altered internally a great deal over the years, and the façade, with its carved badges of the Royal Artillery and the Royal Engineers over the entrance, is almost the only unchanged part of the Barracks. Nowadays Blighmont is the base of the Territorial Army's Royal Artillery and Military Hospitals training units.

In the period just before the outbreak of the war, Southampton had seen a build up of troops and equipment in the docks, but the events of 1940 completely changed the situation. After the fall of France to the Germans, Southampton became more vulnerable to attack, and in view of a possible invasion the port was closed to all but coastal ships. The bombing of 1940 and 1941 damaged many warehouses and transit sheds in the port, there were 69 raids affecting the docks, but the quays and dry docks escaped serious damage. In 1942 the port was re-opened for the 'lease-lend' cargoes of food and essential materials from America.

As the war dragged on and entered its final crucial stages, Millbrook was to play a vital part in the preparations for the invasion of Europe, Operation Overlord. Planning for D-Day began as early as 1943. It was soon realised that the invading forces would need to take their own harbours with them if they were ever to get the vast amount of essential equipment ashore in France. So Naval designers came up with the idea of Mulberry harbours. These consisted of huge concrete 'Phoenix' caissons supported on legs, or 'spuds' as they were called. These structures were to be linked up to form platforms which could go up and down with the tides.

I was told an interesting story about the derivation of the name 'Mulberry' harbour. The Admiralty took over the premises of Kingswood School, Lansdowne

American troops at Berth 107 in the New Docks embarking on D-Day. The spire of Millbrook Church is visible on the far left of the picture and Toogood's warehouse is partly hidden by the barrage balloon. *Hallett Jerrard Collection, Southampton City Cultural Services.*

Hill, in Bath, as the Headquarters for the design of Naval equipment. In the garden of the school was an ancient mulberry tree, which inspired the name for the harbour being designed there. After the war the engineers and naval architects left behind a cartoon, embellished with mulberry leaves and fruit, depicting various bits of equipment in a seashore setting. The cartoon is still in the school's possession. This information was given to me by John Evans, a past pupil of the school, and although a researcher has recently called the story into question, it has certainly been part of the school's lore for over half a century.

Southampton became the major Mulberry harbour construction centre in the country, in particular the King George V Graving Dock in Millbrook. Berths 105–7 in the New Docks were used to harbour flotillas of landing craft and a new railway depot was laid out to enable trains to be shipped over to France after the initial invasion.

In the summer of 1943 an American Unit, Headquarters 14th Port, arrived to organise the handling of cargoes of equipment. A huge American encampment appeared on Green Park in Millbrook, and the War Office requisitioned Millbrook Recreation ground. On 31 March 1944, Regulated Area No. 2 Order was issued and the southern counties of the British Isles came under a blanket of secrecy, travel was restricted and areas of the countryside were put out of bounds,

particularly near the coast. Guards were posted at railway stations and bus depots and barriers were set up on roads entering the zone from outside. There were tank traps and a guard post in Millbrook Road and more 'dragon's teeth' in Oakley Road.

Of course this was all happening very close to the homes of Millbrook residents, it could hardly be kept secret from them.

John Northcott was a schoolboy for most of the war, not being called up for the Navy until 1944. He lived at the bottom end of Regents Park Road, so he was well placed to see the construction work going on around the Graving Dock.

"By the time I came home on leave to Southampton again they were preparing for the invasion of France, D-Day, and parts of the Mulberry Harbours were being built in the King George V Graving Dock. Security and secrecy were very important because they didn't want the Germans to find out what was going on. Sometimes German planes were sent over on reconnaissance missions, and to prevent them taking photographs there were smoke canisters along Regents Park Road. They were like dustbins and were set about 100 yards apart and linked by electrical wire. If some unidentified plane came over they could be triggered and would release a smoke screen to drift across the Dock. It didn't do people with asthma much good!"

The arrival of large numbers of American troops on their doorstep in Green Park was certainly a novelty for Millbrook villagers. The Americans had smarter uniforms, plenty of rations, more money to spend, and were generous with gifts of food, sweets, chewing gum and nylon stockings.

Edna De la Cour remembered her contact with the American soldiers:

"With the war still in progress we learned not to expect any luxuries in the way of food or clothing. Everything was rationed. Even so, we were luckier than most families inasmuch that Dad had contacts with a few friendly Yankee cookhouse boys billeted at the American bases where he had contracts to collect daily kitchen waste for his pigs. The Americans wanted for nothing, and consequently little packages would often be smuggled into Dad's lorry camouflaged by cabbage leaves or the like, perhaps a small block of real butter, a handful of sweets, a few slices of bacon etc. When Dad arrived home with these luxuries there was great excitement, but we were sworn to secrecy. Sometimes freshly baked loaves of bread would be stacked in cardboard boxes, the cooks had to dispose of anything surplus to the troops' requirements. After rescuing enough for our own larder, Mum would offer some of this bounty to neighbours. Many units of the American Armed Forces were stationed all around us, including a camp in our beloved Green Park, and it was inevitable that off-duty soldiers swarmed in our streets like a plague of ants. As Mary and I were still only ten and twelve years of age, we escaped any unwelcome attention, but it was a great attraction for the local young ladies to socialise with the GIs. No doubt many favours were exchanged for precious commodities like nylon stockings, cigarettes and so on."

In the weeks just before D-Day there was a huge build-up of both British and American troops awaiting embarkation for France. Tanks and lorries were parked nose to tail in the streets, giving the householders the opportunity of befriending the soldiers. Many people invited them into their homes to share meals or wash clothes and have baths.

John Northcott vividly remembered this.

"As D-Day got closer hundreds of tanks and army lorries were stacked in the streets all around us awaiting embarkation for France, every empty space had a tank in it. There was a tank right outside our house, practically in the front garden, people befriended the soldiers and often invited them into their homes. One day I came home from work and there was a huge Red Indian sitting in the front room eating pickled onions, wearing American Army uniform of course, not a feathered headdress. Then they disappeared quite suddenly and we heard that the invasion of France was taking place."

Edna De la Cour also watched these events unfolding.

"A few days before D-Day, 6 June 1944, there started a huge build-up of troops ready for the mass exodus to the Normandy beaches. Every road into Southampton was blocked with the movement of vehicles and men, none more so than Redbridge Road because so many personnel of all nationalities had been camping in the New Forest in readiness for the all-important battle. For forty-eight hours we watched convoy after convoy, an unbroken stream of tanks, gun carriers and lorries wending their way towards the docks. The noise was deafening as the tanks ripped up the asphalt road, and all onlookers were in tears as we witnessed the grim faces of the poor lads. Many thousands never came back. At one point, when everything ground to a halt, Mum frantically made piles of sandwiches which were gratefully accepted."

Then at last, on 8 May 1945, the war in Europe was over, and although victory over Japan was not achieved until August 1945, people felt able to celebrate. **Edna De la Cour** again describes her feelings on that day.

"After six years of hardship and long separations it is easy to understand the fever of excitement and celebration madness that broke out when victory was declared. It was as if a heavy shroud had been lifted from everyone's shoulders. On VE Day from noon onwards, after years of silence, the church bells rang out again."

The Sunday after VE day was designated a day of national thanksgiving and arrangements were made for a special United Service at Millbrook. A combined service for all was held at Holy Trinity Church at 3.30 p.m. It was preceded by a parade, which assembled at the old school in Wimpson Lane and then marched to the church. It included as many representatives of His Majesty's services as were available, together with Civil Defence workers, the Fire Service, Home Guard, nurses, and all aspects of the national effort.

After the end of hostilities life began to return to normal. Although the blackout had been partly relaxed since September 1944, now it could be completely abandoned. Green Park was handed back to Millbrook Parish Council for public use on 31 January 1945, "Needless to say the War Office have left it in a very bad condition," complained the Parish Clerk. Some jobs took a long time, the public air-raid shelter in Maybush was not demolished until 1948. Discussions took place about a Millbrook War Memorial and were abandoned as being too expensive.

In 1944 it was suggested by the British Legion that war memorials should take the form of some sort of public building, not a stone cross which was of no use to the community. Millbrook Parish Council proposed that a public library should be built at Maybush

The Millbrook Parish Book of Remembrance for those who lost their lives in the service of their country 1914–1918 and 1939–1945. St. Peter's Church, Maybush. *Photograph Rosaleen Wilkinson.*

Corner as a war memorial, "which will act not only as a tribute to those who have paid the supreme sacrifice but as a social amenity and a place of learning and knowledge so that future wars may be avoided." However, in 1946 the Council decided that raising £2,000 by public subscription for the memorial library would be too difficult and it would not be proceeded with. Eventually a more modest memorial was decided upon, a Book of Remembrance to commemorate the dead of both World Wars. This is kept on display at St. Peter's Church, Maybush.

The Victory thanksgiving service was one of the last events which Millbrook celebrated as a real village community. Within a few years the village would be obliterated in order to make a better road system.

It seems very strange that no protests were made about the road plans, considering the implications they had for the villagers. There were no petitions or banner waving processions, the community just seems to have accepted its fate. Centuries old inns, thatched cottages, the Elizabethan manor house, elegant Victorian mansions, terraced homes, farmhouses, were all demolished. Perhaps the years of wartime had conditioned people into an unquestioning acceptance of official decrees or perhaps people really wanted a fresh start after the war. Whatever the reason, the old Millbrook, which had survived the dangers of the Blitz, was cleared away, and the villagers dispersed to new homes.

BIBLIOGRAPHY

Southampton and D-Day – Oral History Archive, Southampton City Heritage.

Burton, Lesley: *D-Day, Our Great Enterprise.*

Millbrook parish magazines 1935–57 – Southampton City Archives.

Air-raid Precautions Committee SC2/3/39 1 and 2 – Southampton City Archives.

Evacuation correspondence 10/14/11 – Southampton City Archives.

Absorbed parishes, Millbrook to Southampton and Parish record book SC/AM – Southampton City Archives.

CHAPTER XIV

The Millbrook Park Estate

During the Second World War, not only was Southampton town centre devastated by bombing, but 4,278 homes had been totally destroyed, in addition to the thousands of other houses badly damaged. Even before the war ended the Council was planning for the future. Under the guidance of James Matthews, the Borough of Southampton prepared a development plan which saw a vision of a modern garden city with spacious parks, housing estates, shopping centres and schools. The plan sought to provide sites for new industries and provide housing for the expected increase in population.

The development of the Millbrook Park Council Estate is very much bound up with the story of the incorporation of Millbrook into Southampton, and the first mention of the plan is in the proceedings of the Parish Council on 21 July 1944. The chairman reported to the Council meeting:

"The future of Millbrook now seems to be coming to a head and my Council has received a plan from Southampton Corporation in which they propose to acquire all available land. The Parish Council view the only solution is for Millbrook to be incorporated before development is commenced. It would be most unfair to expect present ratepayers to foot the bill for additional services for an influx of Southampton People, or to use the Parish Council as a stop gap."

The Parish Council wrote officially to Southampton Corporation objecting to the compulsory purchase of land in October 1945.

"No alternative provision is being made for smallholders for land they now occupy and use for their livelihood, who would be dispossessed by the proposal. There would be loss of allotments. The proposal would mean the whole parish is to be acquired, except for a few small built-up areas, and to be covered with houses, making a township in the area of another authority."

However, not everybody objected to the proposal.

Mr F. G. Elmes, Chairman of Millbrook Parish Council, in his report to the annual meeting at the schoolroom in Wimpson Methodist Chapel, said:

"I feel that for a parish the size of Millbrook still to be attached to a rural district is wrong. The parishioners would gain much from incorporation into the borough. They could look forward to having good street lighting, a better bus service, more shops, improved road maintenance. They would like to have regular refuse collection and connection to the main sewer."

In many ways, Mr. Elmes was quite right, Millbrook lacked many modern services, despite being so close to such a large town as Southampton. The boxes of Parish Council correspondence, held in Southampton Archives, are crammed full of letters from angry parishioners complaining about their overflowing cesspits, only emptied once a month. Other letters ask for pot-holes in the roads to be attended to, or complain that the gas lamp at the corner of the road has been faulty for weeks. Even in the 1950s Millbrook still had a lamplighter who toured the roads switching on the street lamps individually.

A Public Enquiry was held in December 1945. The Deputy Town Clerk of Southampton said that there were 8,644 applications for housing accommodation. The land was required for houses for the homeless. During the war 4,000 houses were destroyed, 36,000 damaged and for six years no new houses had been built. All areas around the town had been considered and the land to the west of Southampton was most suitable. Practically all the land in the proposed area at Millbrook was in the ownership of Mr. Barker-Mill, who had stated he was willing to sell land to the Corporation.

Mr Roe said that the land was agricultural land and there were bound to be cases of hardship. Of the objections lodged, 25 were lodged on hardship grounds. The Council sympathised and would do all they could to ease the burden, but individual cases of hardship could not be allowed to obstruct the Council in their housing plans any more than they had done in the war. He added:

"Our greatest sympathy must be with the thousands of people without homes. I can give parishioners assurances that they will not be turned out of their houses without being offered suitable alternative accommodation. When the land is developed those who have shops now will be given reasonable opportunity to carry on their trade on the Council Estate. To smallholders and farmers, I cannot offer any alternative accommodation apart from the houses in which they reside."

It was quite clear that protests by the Parish Council would be useless. Southampton over-rode the local Council and in 1948 took responsibility for all applications for council housing in Millbrook. Despite the fact that, over the years, the Parish Council had provided fifty of its own council houses, Millbrook parishioners were not to be given any preference. The homes would go into the housing pool and be allocated on a 'points' basis to anyone who applied. Then in March 1949, the Town Clerk of Southampton informed the Parish Council of a decision taken at a meeting of officials in London. Where boroughs, like Southampton, had suffered extensive war damage and were intending to build outside their boundaries, special concessions would be given to take over the land by interim order without waiting for Government approval of the recommendations of the Boundary Commission. By this time, work on the Estate had already started. Plans were in hand for a major development at Millbrook for a housing estate designed in a spacious, garden-city tradition to provide 3,217 homes.

In November 1951 the Millbrook Parish Council set out the conditions they would try to impose on the transfer of power.

1. A complete sewer system for the parish within three years.
2. A system of street lighting within two years.
3. A public library within two years.
4. A public hall within two years.
5. A system of municipal transport within one year.
6. Development of the foreshore at Redbridge for bathing and boating.
7. Installation of public conveniences.
8. Preservation of trees at Green Park.
9. Housing of a parish war memorial.
10. Equality of council house rents.
11. Reservation of space at the cemetery for Millbrook parishioners.
12. Open space at Maybush.

Another Public Enquiry was held in April 1953. Later the *Echo* reported:

"On June 4th 1953, Col. Rhodes, the Ministry Inspector, attended at the Civic Centre. He explored maps and met dignitaries from Southampton and Millbrook Councils, and toured the parish accompanied by the Chairman and Clerk of the Parish Council. Thus ended the Ministry Enquiry into the commencement of a new era in the history of the ancient parish of Millbrook, of which records can be traced from the year A.D. 956."

A few months after this the newspaper carried the public notice which officially ended the status of Millbrook as an independent parish.

"The Southampton (alteration of boundaries) Order 1954.

Notice is hereby given that by the above order the Millbrook Parish Council is dissolved from March 31st 1954. All communications usually sent to the Council should after that date be made to the Southampton Borough Council at the Civic Centre, Southampton."

The way was now clear for the wholesale development of Millbrook, and the complete destruction of the ancient community.

The planning of the Millbrook Park Council Estate started in 1946 with the appointment of two engineers, Mr Robson and Mr Charles Shilley. The land for the site, some 500 acres in extent, was purchased from the Barker-Mill estate, and the first phase of building started between Wimpson Lane and Oakley Road.

Charles Shilley, one of the engineers, was interviewed for the Millbrook Oral History Project in 1987 and he gave an interesting account of the development of the estate:

"Tebourba Way and Millbrook Roundabout and the wide road through Millbrook, simply did not exist then. The narrow Millbrook Road was the road to the New Forest, coupled with Wimpson Lane being the main trunk road through from London and Winchester to the Forest and beyond. The area was not built up at all, there was just a little rural development along Millbrook Road and a few houses around the Swan Inn and a few shops and a transport café that served the very limited number of commercial vehicles that used the road. The whole area was outside the Borough at that time. We had to make agreements with various authorities, and farmers had to be given compensation to retire or buy farms elsewhere. A lot of agricultural land was taken and that required permission from the Ministry of Agriculture and Fisheries, it was just after the war and there were still food shortages.

"The Borough architects involved in the design of the homes and the layout and plans were Mr Winston and later Mr Leon Berger. The use of steel, timber and cement was strictly controlled and work could only proceed when materials were available. There was a feeling of great urgency to provide homes after the war and we brought in industrialised housing, that is making units of the houses off-site and bringing them in and assembling them. Cornish

The early stages of road development, probably about 1950, the proposed line of Tebourba Way is shown as a hatched line. *Photograph courtesy of* Southern Daily Echo.

units, Reema houses and Wates houses were all types of industrial housing. Some temporary homes were also set up using Prefabs, they were single storey bungalow-type houses, very compact. Of course there was a labour shortage after the war too and German Prisoners of War were used on the Prefab sites. There was also an apprenticeship scheme, which took boys straight from school to build the more conventional brick houses. The tempo of development really picked up when the factory built units were introduced and flats started to be put up. In 1949 there were 350 homes completed, in 1950 around 700, and in 1952 over 1,000 homes.

"The emphasis was on providing housing units and the Government dictated what types of units and materials you could use. Bricks and traditional building materials were in such short supply after the war that an order for them might take a year to come through. Authorities which were 'go-ahead', like Southampton, were trying to get the maximum number of houses built for people on their waiting lists so they had to use the materials which were more readily available. In order to meet housing targets the concrete units just had to be used. We discovered the problems of deterioration with these materials some forty years later, but at the time they

seemed the reasonable solution to our difficulties.

"Housing development proceeded so fast that no shops were provided for the first residents. The area was served by mobile shops or temporary shops in old war-time Nissen huts. Various traders had licences to provide facilities on site, such as a chemist, grocer, butcher and newsagent. A major retail outlet was not provided until the 1960s.

The new shopping centre in Kendal Avenue. *Southampton City Archives.*

102

"When the estate was built there was no provision at all of community facilities, there was no central point where things could happen, not even a hut for meetings. Eventually the community did establish itself, indirectly through the activities of the churches and the British Legion and political parties and the pubs that were on the outskirts of the area. Initially children even had to go to schools on the periphery of the estate. People had to do things very much for themselves. In 1953 the residents of the Prefabs wanted to hold a Coronation tea party, they made house to house collections for the food, but there was just nowhere to have it indoors if the weather was bad. In the end the celebrations had to be held in a hall two miles away at Christmas! It was only with the development of the community facilities in Redbridge School that anything other than self-generated social activities really made progress. There was no scope for private enterprise commercial development either, nobody could put up a restaurant or dance hall because the estate was all part and parcel of an overall local authority plan.

"The Millbrook estate is very spaciously laid out with lots of green areas. This was partly because of the planning regulations about density and open spaces in force at the time, but the physical layout of the Millbrook estate with its wide-open spaces is not particularly conducive to close community feelings. The land had previously been fields with hedgerows and magnificent old oak trees marking the boundaries and it was thought desirable to retain these large trees. In many places houses were located carefully to avoid the trees and set back 60 or 70 feet from the road. Sadly, once all the drainage work for the housing was completed, the water table in this very saturated area fell and took the water away from these massive oaks. Within ten years hardly one remained.

"In the 1950s 12 to 14 houses per acre was considered quite close development, now (i.e. in 1987) 20 per acre is more usual, and with flats it can be as many as thirty-three units of dwellings. Nobody could have predicted the increase of car ownership, which has led to severe parking problems on the estate. In 1950 regulations laid down one parking space per 20 dwellings on developments of terraced or semi-detached houses. Today, some of the three-bedroom houses can have as many as four cars attached to them, the family car, the wife's car and the two grown up children's cars. Standards at the time specified the construction of 13-foot wide roads, so there are great difficulties now with roadside parking on these comparatively narrow roads.

Millbrook Roundabout 1954. There is a large group of prefabs next to the new Tebourba Way, and the Millbrook Industrial Estate is beginning to develop. *Photograph courtesy of* Southern Daily Echo.

"There were certain problems over the roads, which were becoming inadequate for the traffic, especially Wimpson Lane. In order for development of the estate to progress a new road had to be built from Winchester Road to Millbrook to replace Wimpson Lane as the main trunk road. Southampton Borough Council agreed to construct a new road to a similar standard to the existing Wimpson Lane, but of course that was a very low standard. The Lane was narrow and just had ditches on either side, sufficient for pre-war traffic. The new road was only open three months before the sub-base started to give way and the road had to be closed off and re-built to a much higher standard."

The new road was named Tebourba Way in honour of the Hampshire Regiment's part in the World War II battle of Tebourba. It was officially opened in 1953. This is the plaque which stands at the junction of Tebourba Way and Oakley Road:

TEBOURBA WAY

WAS OPENED ON APRIL 30th 1953 BY

THE WORSHIPFUL THE MAYOR OF
SOUTHAMPTON

(ALDERMAN E. BURROWS)

AND SO NAMED IN RECOGNITION OF THE

BRAVERY OF THE MEN OF THE

ROYAL HAMPSHIRE REGIMENT

WHO TOOK PART IN THE
BATTLE OF TEBOURBA

NORTH AFRICA, DECEMBER 1942

Mr Shilley continues:

"The old Millbrook Road was very narrow and dangerous; it was about as wide as the service road in front of Holy Trinity Church. When the road was widened the Royal Mail public house and the Oliver Cromwell had to be pulled down. There was considerable heartache when the Oliver Cromwell had to go because it was a very old established coaching inn. The Manor House was demolished at this time as well. The new highway also opened the way for development of the industrial estates, the Waste Paper Company was one of the earliest businesses established.

"The Millbrook roundabout was built in 1963 to take the access to Tebourba Way, Wimpson Lane, Redbridge Road and Millbrook Road, and this provided the forerunner of the whole western approach road. The Redbridge roundabout was built in 1964 with the general idea that the Millbrook Road would become the main approach to Southampton from the west, supplying the container port and industrial area on that side of the city. It would eventually link up with the motorway network at Redbridge. The Millbrook and Redbridge flyovers were completed in the late 1970s and linked to the city network via Mountbatten Way.

"The development of the docks started in the 1930s and a lot of land was reclaimed for this. Access to Millbrook foreshore was more and more restricted by the docks and warehousing. The building of the container port in the late 1970s led to more land reclamation and the disappearance of the beach."

In 1986 the Millbrook Oral History Project was set up to capture a 'snap-shot' of ordinary people's lives. These are some extracts from the tape-recorded interviews which various residents gave about their lives on the estate. They are anonymous. (*Extracts courtesy of Oral History Archive, Southampton City Council.*)

"We moved in to the house in October 1949. It was

Millbrook Roundabout, January 1968.
Photograph by G. E. C. Webb.

Some of the early council houses. *Southampton City Archives.*

opposite the Chest Hospital on the corner of Oakley Road, there was no Tebourba Way. It was one of the first homes built and we could tell there had been a farm there before because we were still getting rid of mice for quite a while, little field mice. [This was the site of Mousehole Farm, and that area was called Mousehole.] But it was lovely for the children, so free and easy, at first it was nearer the village atmosphere."

"We moved in brand new. In the kitchen was a unit with an enamel sink, no cupboards, you put curtains along the front. There was a coke boiler for hot water. There was a gas poker to light the fire in the sitting room. We had three bedrooms and an L-shaped lounge with lino on the floor. The rent collector came round every week, it was 23 shillings (£1.15p)."

"We had to be careful with money, we had little jam jars with labels on. There was a jar for rent, a jar for electricity, one for gas, one for food, one for clothing and an emergency jar."

For some people the move to Millbrook represented an escape from really squalid housing conditions.

"I was born in 1946 and we moved to Millbrook when I was six in 1952. Where we lived before in St. Mary's we had no running water and no gas. We had a pump in the garden and Mum cooked on the fire. We had a galvanised bath in the kitchen. There were rats and mice all over the place.

"At our house in Maybush Road we had a reasonable size garden. Dad partitioned a piece with trellis-work and he made a nice lawn and red roses round the trellis. All round the back we had our own vegetables, which was really quite new.

"We had a 20 foot lounge/diner, kitchen, hall, two

bedrooms and a bathroom. We had the open fire and nobody wanted to leave it, it was cold everywhere else in the winter. We were careful with the decorations, I mean, we weren't quite into the Land of Plenty.

"Don't touch! Those things cost a lot of money.

"Mother had a fridge, they were huge in the 1950s, and a boiler to do the washing, and a wringer, no washing machine.

"At first I went to the Green Lane school, it must have been a temporary thing until they built a school on the estate. Green Lane was all ditches and bushes and kids could hide and jump out at you. When Newlands School was built they split us up, half went to Newlands and half stayed at Millbrook.

"Mother always made my clothes and woolies, which I hated. In my teenage years the fashion was hooped petticoats with layers and layers of net. We had 'winkle picker' shoes with stiletto heels, they did harm to the feet and to floors. I didn't wear make-up until I left school, we weren't as adventurous then as children are today. I used to listen to Radio Luxembourg, that was all the thing. I used to have it on late at night under the bedclothes.

"I was in the secretarial stream at school, so there was no real choice about jobs and I got a job as a typist in an Insurance office. Mum made me open a Building Society account when I first started work. I always put in so much a week until I got married and I'd saved £1,000 by then."

Not everyone was delighted with the new housing estate, this young housewife was twenty-four when she moved to Millbrook in 1954.

"When I got off the bus, the first day I came to see the house, I thought I could never live out here, it's like being in the wilderness. There didn't seem to be any life, it was just houses, no proper roads or pavements or lights or anything, and it just seemed so far away from everything. At first I thought it was horrible, like a desolate wilderness. The nearest shops were at Maybush Corner.

"We all moved in at more or less the same time, we were all sort of friendly and had children. Our children grew up together and it was quite a nice little community round here. As the children went to school, so we used to have afternoons free, we'd have an afternoon in my house and have a cup of tea, and then we'd go to another house the next week. We started up the Colne Avenue Young Wives group, there wasn't much to do unless you belonged to a church group."

In March 2001 I talked to **Doreen Pond** about her early years living on the estate.

"When we first moved in we lived in a flat on the corner of Mansel Road. Opposite us, where The Saints pub stands, there used to be an old cottage. We used to see a woman come out of the house and draw her water up from the well in a bucket. When

A view of Section 5 of the estate being built in 1954, you can still see stooks of harvested corn in the fields at the right hand corner of the picture. *Photograph courtesy of* Southern Daily Echo.

the pub had been built she had to leave, and you could see how old the house and everything was when they brought the furniture out. A bit further along Mansel Road there used to be a beautiful thatched farmhouse. [That was Upper Wimpson Farm.]

"When we moved here in 1953, the estate was still being built and the old cottages and farms were still there. Once the cottages had been knocked down the Corporation used the land as a rubbish tip to build it up and make it into a playing field, that area is Mansel Park now. The smell used to come across and we had to shut the windows, it was awful. Then when they stopped dumping the rubbish the gypsies came and camped there, they moved on when Millbrook Towers were built.

"We lived with Eddie's parents when we were first married, they said we could have a room in the house until we got settled down. People often lived with their parents for a while when they got married. When we applied for a Council house they asked all sorts of questions that they don't ask today. They asked if we had any money saved up, could we afford to buy any furniture? I said yes, because if you didn't have the money they didn't let you move. The only thing we had when we first moved in was a bed-settee, and we just got more bits and pieces as we went along. In those days oranges came in big wooden boxes and you could get them from the greengrocer. If you put a little curtain across the front you could make a nice little cupboard. We were very pleased to move out into a place of our own, it was like Buckingham Palace to us then, we were quite happy. The flat had two bedrooms, a small kitchen and bathroom and a living room, and the rent was £1.0s.8d a week. We had a coal fire in the living room with a back-boiler for the hot water, and all the other rooms were stone cold. There were coal sheds out the back of the flats and we had to fetch the coal in buckets from there. We were lucky living on the ground floor, but people who lived in the upper storeys had to carry it all the way up the stairs. There were lots of other young families living round us. They were still building on the estate when the children got a bit older and they used to play on the heaps of builder's sand.

"It seemed lovely and open, like the country, but there were no buses and no shops so I had to walk into Shirley to do the shopping. I had a great big twin pram and four children, two babies inside, one sitting on a seat, and one walking. Those big old prams had a deep well underneath and you could take the babies out, fill it up with groceries, then put the babies back. I would manage all right until I got to the hill outside the Chest Hospital, but then I couldn't push it up the slope and I had to wait for

Millbrook Towers under construction. The 25-storey block was officially opened on 5 May 1965.
Photograph courtesy of Southern Daily Echo.

someone to come along and ask them to help me. Times were hard, but we didn't know any different, we'd always had to work hard. It didn't come as a surprise to us to do what we had to do, we didn't really expect to have buses or telephones laid on.

"We moved up to this house in 1957. This is a three-bedroom house."

I met **Dave Churchill** at a Local History meeting in November 2000 and talked to him about his childhood on Millbrook estate in the 1960s.

"We moved to Pennine Road in the 1960s when I was a child. They say we were brought up in the Swinging Sixties.

"There weren't any proper shops on the estate then, there were Nissen huts. There was one on the corner by 'The Saints' pub, it was like a tin shack where you could get your daily papers and things like that. Then there were huts in Cumbrian Way where you could buy groceries. I can remember being sent down to get big tins of National Dried Milk and thick orange juice for my little brother, that was in another Nissen hut in Cumbrian Way, it must have been a health centre or something.

"Our house was a three-bedroom terrace house. I had a brother and a sister younger than me. We had open fires, and in the summer I used to go out with a little cart collecting firewood so that we had a good bunker full for the winter. My Dad would never buy the coal in the summer at the cheaper prices, he'd wait until we needed it in the cold weather, but I liked to feel that at least we'd got a nice lot of wood stored up to keep us warm. I got most of the wood from the old prefabs at the bottom of Tebourba Way. A lot of prefabs were built there after the War, but by the sixties, except for a few gypsy families, most of the people had moved out into proper houses, and they were derelict. So I used to go and break up bits of wood from them. British Oxygen built a factory there when the prefabs were cleared, and now it's Homebase and the Superbowl."

[Pre-fabricated houses were single storey units

Temporary shops in Cumbrian Way. The three 'funnels' on the roof of Mason Moor Primary School can be seen behind the building. *Southampton City Archives.*

Eileen Downes (centre, in cardigan) and friends in 1959. Notice their identical brown sandals, just like the ones mentioned by Dave Churchill!

providing basic accommodation for families. They were made of an asbestos type material in sections and could be assembled quite quickly. They had a kitchen, bathroom, living room and usually two bedrooms.]

"We weren't the only ones who were short of money. There wasn't much affluence where I came from, there weren't many cars. I don't remember it being very smart, we were all in the same boat you know, brown sandals from Woolworth's for the six weeks holiday in summer and new shoes to go back to school. People had jobs then, they were affluent times in the sixties with low unemployment, but they were low paid jobs. Mum was a school dinner-lady. My Dad was a carpenter and he worked seven days a week, but he spent too much of his wages in the pub. That happened to quite a few families. Mum and Dad weren't really interested in our schooling at all, we didn't have much mental stimulation at home, but I didn't misbehave at school. They didn't worry about planning for the future, with Dad it was a case of 'easy come, easy go', although he did buy our TV set rather than wasting money on renting one like most people did. It was the old black and white TV in those days of course. We didn't have a fridge, I can remember putting the milk outside in a bucket of water in the summer, but the milk still went off if you didn't put fresh cold water in as it got warm. Mum had a washing machine, but she wouldn't use it because she said it cost too much. She used to wash everything by hand and just use it as a spin dryer.

"In the evenings we didn't do much as kids, just played in the wood and climbed trees, or played football. Every year on November 5th there used to be a big bonfire on the corner of Wimpson Lane, and the Council or the Forestry people would come and bring wood that they didn't want and make a huge pile for us. One year some kids smashed up trees

growing in the playing fields to put on the bonfire, so the Council came and took the whole pile away as a punishment."

I spoke to two members of the Millbrook Local History Society, who were both brought up on the estate and still live there. I asked them about their childhood memories from the 1950s and '60s, and how they feel about the estate now.

Eileen Downes is chairman of the Millbrook Local History Society, a former parent governor of Millbrook Community School and chairman of the Parent Teacher Association.

Maureen Harvey, is a parent governor of Millbrook Community School, and the former secretary of the Parent Teacher Association.

Eileen – "My parents got the key to the house in Kendal Avenue in 1953 when I was just a baby, it was our first proper family home, not just living in rooms any more."

Maureen – My family moved into a flat near Mansel School at first, and then to a house in Durlston Road. Eventually I took on the tenancy of that house, so I'm back in the home where I was brought up.
   "When we were children all the trees on the estate were still little, everything was very green, and hardly anyone had a car. They didn't envisage people having cars, especially if they lived on a council estate."

Eileen – "One neighbour had a motor bike and sidecar, that was really flash."

Maureen – "Some people had push-bikes or scooters and mopeds to get to work."

Eileen – "You had to walk quite a long way to get to the bus stop . You never had to worry about safety, in the holidays a whole gang of us would push off about nine o'clock in the morning with a few sandwiches and spend the whole day playing in 'Bluebell Wood' and come home when we were hungry."

Maureen – "We used to go to the cornfields where Test Playing Fields are now. The corn used to be full of blue cornflowers. Beyond that there was Hurst's piggery. We used to go along a footpath through the fields to get to the River Test, the 'Wibbies' as we used to call it."

Eileen – "I think 'wibbies' means willows or hazels."

Maureen – "Everybody got told off for going there because the current was so strong in the river.
   "When we were teenagers we used to go to Millbrook and Maybush Youth Club during the week. There was a Junior Club, which was finished by 8 o'clock, and after that the Senior Club for the over fourteens. There was a canteen where we took it in turn to cook, there was a quiet room for chatting, and a third room for table tennis, pin ball

machines and all sorts of games. We used to have all the latest records blaring out. We used to have the Beatles up at Millbrook but down at Wimpson they played Diana Ross, the Isley Brothers, the Four Tops, Otis Redding. On Fridays and Saturdays Wimpson Youth Club was the place to be seen. The majority of Millbrook girls married Millbrook boys. If you looked at the people who lived on the estate, you would probably find that about fifty per cent of them were living here when we were children, they've been here all those years."

Eileen – "The houses themselves on the estate are very nice, they've been modernised, we've got central heating, the gardens are a good size. Millbrook is the greenest estate in Southampton and there's plenty of space for children to play.

"In the papers you read about vandalism and crime, burnt out cars, rubbish all over the place and so on, but it isn't always like that on the estate. The majority of people who live on the estate are honest, decent, ordinary people like ourselves. I've visited lots of parents in their own homes in connection with my work in a local school, and people here have the same hopes and aspirations for their children as people who live in more affluent areas of the town, only sometimes we've just got to fight a bit harder for things. We've got to change the perception of living on the estate, that it smacks of 'second best'.

"I like living in Millbrook for the good community spirit, good neighbours and friends that I've made over the years. I'm proud to call myself a Millbrook girl."

BIBLIOGRAPHY

Oral History Archive – Southampton City Council Cultural Services.

Absorbed parishes, Millbrook to Southampton and Parish record book SC/AM – Southampton City Archives.

Millbrook Parish Council Letters SC/AM 112–5 – Southampton City Archives.

Index